WILD ANIMALS
I HAVE KNOWN

WILD ANIMALS
I HAVE KNOWN

ERNEST THOMPSON SETON

Adapted by
Ardis E. Burton

Edited by
William Kottmeyer
St. Louis Public Schools

Illustrated by
Robert S. Robison

Phoenix Learning Resources
New York

The Phoenix Everyreaders

The EVERYREADERS were selected from the great literature of the world and adapted to the needs of today's children. This series retains the flavor of the originals, providing mature content and dramatic plot structure, along with eye appeal designed to motivate reading.

This approach was first developed in the renowned St. Louis Reading Clinic by Dr. Kottmeyer and is the direct outgrowth of wide and successful teaching of remedial reading.

A high interest level plus the carefully controlled vocabulary and sentence structure enable pupils to read the stories easily, confidently, and with enjoyment.

ISBN 0-7915-1359-9

3 4 5 6 7 8 9 0 99 98 97 96 95 94

Contents

Old Lobo, King of the Wolves   1

Silverspot, the Story of a Crow   23

Raggylug, the Story of a
     Cottontail Rabbit   31

Wully, the Story of a Yellow Dog   57

Red Ruff, the Story of a Partridge   69

The Springfield Fox   95

The Pacing Mustang   113

PART 1

OLD LOBO
King of the Wolves

The Corrumpa Valley is a large grazing land in northern New Mexico, named for the Corrumpa River. Many sheep and cattle feed on this grassy land. At one time, the wicked king of the Corrumpa was an old gray wolf named Lobo.

Lobo and his pack of gray wolves hunted in the Corrumpa Valley for many years. The ranchers knew them well. Lobo was a giant wolf. He was very smart. His voice was easy to tell from the voices of other wolves. When Old Lobo's deep voice boomed, the ranchers knew that they would soon find freshly killed sheep or cattle.

Old Lobo's pack was a small one, but each wolf in his pack became a famous killer. During the last part of his life, he had only five followers. One of these was a beautiful white wolf called Blanca. She was Lobo's mate.

Lobo's pack was well known to the ranchers. All of them would gladly have paid for the hide of any one of these wolves. But no one could catch one of them.

Lobo and his pack would not eat poisoned bait. They stayed out of the wolf traps. In five years they killed more than two thousand of the finest cows and sheep in the Corrumpa. They often killed sheep for the fun of it. One night alone they killed two hundred fifty sheep without eating any.

This was no starving pack of killers. Lobo's wolves were well fed and fat. They would not eat an animal that had died of old age or sickness. For fear they would be poisoned, they would not eat an animal some rancher had killed. Seldom did they kill a horse. They liked best the tender parts of a freshly killed calf.

The ranchers tried many things to get rid of this pack of killers. They put a great price on Lobo's head. They put out many kinds of poisoned bait. But Lobo was always too smart for the ranchers. He and his pack ate only what they killed themselves.

A WISE OLD LEADER

Lobo and his pack had never been known to attack a human being. If they saw a man, even far away, they would run. They knew guns and feared them.

One time a cowboy heard Lobo's voice close by. He got off his horse and crept over a little hilltop. From the top he saw Lobo's pack. The wolves had rounded up a small herd of cattle. Lobo sat by himself. Blanca and the others were trying to get a fat young cow away from the herd. The cattle stood close together in a circle with their heads outward. Their horns pointed at the wolves. The wolves could not reach the young cow.

Finally Lobo jumped up and ran toward the cattle. He roared and showed his teeth.

The cattle were frightened. They ran here and there. The fat young cow also ran. Before she had gone twenty steps Lobo was upon her. He grabbed her by the neck and threw her to the ground. Lobo turned over with her, but quickly leaped to his feet. Then the wolf pack killed her. Lobo himself took no part in the killing.

"Now, why couldn't some of you have done that without wasting so much time?" he seemed to say, as he sat back watching.

The cowboy mounted his horse and rode up to the wolves. They ran away. He poisoned the cow's body in three places, hoping that the wolves would come back to eat their kill. The next morning he rode back. He hoped to find some of the pack dead from the poison.

The wolves had eaten the cow, all right. But they had carefully cut out and thrown aside each of the poisoned parts.

Each year the ranchers put a larger price on Lobo's head. Finally they offered one thousand dollars for Lobo, dead or alive. A young Texas Ranger named Tannerey heard about this large reward. One day he came galloping up the trail of the Corrumpa. He had fine horses, good guns, and a large pack of wolfhounds. He was ready to get Lobo.

This man and his wolfhounds had already killed many wolves on the Texas plains. He thought that he would have Lobo's hide hanging from his saddle in a few days.

Away went Tannerey one summer morning. His wolfhounds jumped with joy. They knew they were on the trail of another killer wolf. Before they had gone two miles, they saw Lobo's band.

The job of wolfhounds is to overtake the wolves and hold them until the hunter rides up and shoots the wolves. This had been easy for Tannerey's pack on the Texas plains. But they did not know Old Lobo.

The rocky trails of the Corrumpa River wind around, and it is easy to get lost. Led by Lobo, the gray pack ran for the trails. One wolf went one way; another went another way. Several dogs followed one wolf. This was just what the wolves wanted. Their trick was to turn on the hounds. One wolf can take care of two or three hounds.

That night, when the chase was over, Tannerey called his wolfhounds together. Only six of them came back, and one of the six was badly wounded. Tannerey tried two more times to get Lobo and his pack. On his last try, his best horse was killed in a fall. Tannerey had failed. He gave up and went back to Texas, and Lobo still ruled the Corrumpa Valley.

The next year two more hunters came to try their luck. Each one wanted to win the thousand dollars. The first man had made a new poison. He had found a new way to set it out. The second man believed that Old Lobo was a ghost wolf, a devil. This man tried charms and magic spells as well as poison.

No matter what trick they tried, Lobo figured it out. No matter how strong the poison, Lobo never tasted it. And, since Old Lobo was not a ghost, the magic charms did not work. In all this time, Lobo and his pack never missed a meal. They made their kill each day and lived on the fattest cows. These two hunters gave up at last.

Old Lobo and Blanca built their den that summer not a thousand yards from the house where another hunter lived. Lobo lived with his family, killed cattle, sheep, and even dogs, and seemed to laugh at the hunter's traps and poisons.

"There's where he lived all last summer," the hunter said to me when I got to the Corrumpa. "I couldn't do a thing to him. He just made a fool of me. Lobo is a smart one!"

I MEET THE KING OF THE CORRUMPA

Before I went to the Corrumpa, I could hardly believe all the things I heard about Lobo and his pack. At last I got to know him for myself. A rancher I knew in the Corrumpa asked me to come to New Mexico to try to get rid of this pack of wolves. I was glad to be asked. I wanted to meet Lobo and his band.

As soon as I got there, I spent some time riding around the country to learn all about it. After I had ridden around, I saw that chasing Lobo's pack with wolfhounds and horses would be useless. The wolf pack knew the country better than any man could. I knew I could not outsmart the wolves in a chase. I decided that my traps were too small to catch them. I set to work with poison.

I was set on catching this devil-wolf, as the ranchers called him. There were no poisons that I did not try. Morning after morning I rode out to see what luck I had had. It was always the same: Lobo was too smart for me. I need not tell you all the things I tried. Here is just one case that will show how smart he was.

An old trapper had given me an idea that I thought might work. I melted some cheese together with the fat of a freshly killed young cow. I cooked this in a dish, cutting it with a knife made of bone so there would be no smell of steel. When the stuff was cool, I cut it up into bits. Into each bit I slipped a big dose of poison. With bits of cheese, I sealed the holes again.

During this whole job I wore a pair of gloves that I had soaked in the cow's hot blood. I did not even breathe on the bait, because I carefully covered up my nose and mouth.

When I had the poisoned bait all ready, I put it into a rawhide bag. I had rubbed the bag all over, inside and out, with blood. Then I rode away. I dragged behind me the liver and kidneys of the cow to cover my trail.

Each fourth of a mile I dropped some bait, taking the greatest care not to touch it with my hands. This was on a Monday. I knew that Lobo came to this part of the valley in the early part of each week. I thought I surely had him this time.

"Listen! There he is! I hear him!" cried one of the boys that evening.

Next morning I could hardly wait to see what had happened. Before I had ridden very far, I came on the fresh tracks of the wolves. Lobo's tracks were easy to pick out. A common wolf's forefoot is about four and one-half inches long. But Lobo's was five and one-half inches from claw to heel! Later I found out that he was very large, standing three feet tall at the shoulder and weighing one hundred fifty pounds.

I studied the big tracks and followed the trail of the pack. They had followed my bait. Lobo had found my first piece of bait and picked it up.

"I've got the king at last!" I cried, unable to hide my joy. "I'll find him stiff and dead, within a mile!"

I went on. At last I came to the place where I had dropped the second piece of poisoned bait. It was gone, too.

"Now I know I've got him!" I cried.

I followed Lobo's broad tracks. I stood up in my stirrups, looking ahead. But I could not see any dead wolves. I rode on and on.

The third piece of bait was also gone. I followed Lobo's tracks to the fourth piece of bait. Here I found a most surprising thing. The wise old king had not eaten any bait. He had just carried the pieces all this time in his mouth. Then he had piled the first three pieces of poisoned bait on top of the fourth one and had clawed dirt on them.

That is how Lobo showed what he thought of my trick. After the fourth piece of bait, Lobo and his pack left the trail.

I was sure that poison would never kill this pack of robber wolves. So I got some larger wolf traps. But again Lobo came out on top.

HOW OLD LOBO FOOLED THE TRAPPERS

As I said before, Lobo and his pack killed sheep just for fun. In Corrumpa country, sheep are kept in bands of one to three thousand, under the care of two or three men. At night the sheep are led to a safe place. A man sleeps on each side of the flock.

Sheep are silly. Almost anything will make them run. They follow their leader any place. Ranchers often put half a dozen goats in with a band of sheep. Sheep know that the goats are more careful than they. When something happens, the sheep crowd around the goats.

Lobo knew this. One night two of the men were awakened by the sound of Lobo's attack. The sheep ran to the goats. The goats were not afraid and stood their ground. But no common wolf was leading this attack.

Old Lobo was as smart as the men. He knew that the goats were leaders of the band. He jumped upon the backs of the sheep as they crowded around the goats. He ran over their backs until he came to the goats. Jumping upon them, he began to kill. Soon he had the sheep running. He killed many of them. Many others were lost.

I SET TRAPS FOR LOBO

At last my new wolf traps came. I hired two men to help me set them. We took great care to do the job right and used every trick we knew.

On the second day after we put out our traps, I rode around to see if we had had any luck. I soon came upon Lobo's tracks. They went from trap to trap. I thought I had hidden my traps. I had covered each with dirt. But Lobo had uncovered more than a dozen of them. He had left them, with each trap still set.

"Look here," I said to my helper, pointing to one trap. "He always turns aside in one way. That gives me an idea of how to catch him."

Once again I set my traps. This time they formed an H on the ground: two rows of traps with one between for the crossbar of the H. But this trick did not fool Lobo.

Lobo had come trotting along the trail between the rows of traps. How he knew another trap lay between the two rows, I cannot tell. Why he stopped in time, I do not know. But without turning an inch to right or left, he had slowly and carefully stepped backwards in his own tracks! Then he had come around on the outside of the H. Scratching clods and stones with his hind feet, he had sprung every one of the traps in the H. And so he got away again. He did this many times. No matter how I changed my plan, nothing worked. No plan worked. I began to think that maybe he was a devil-wolf, after all.

THE END OF LOBO

The old gray king of the Corrumpa would have lived many more years, but for a love that caused his downfall.

I saw the tracks of a smaller wolf running ahead of Old Lobo. I could not understand this, but a cowboy made it clear to me.

"I saw them today," he said. "Blanca breaks away from the band, and Lobo goes after her."

"So that's it!" I cried. "Blanca does not obey him. If any of the others did that, Lobo would kill him."

"That's true," the cowboy said. "But he lets Blanca do as she wishes."

Then I thought of a new plan. I killed a cow and cut off the head, which wolves do not touch. Then I put out two traps where they could be seen. I set the head some yards away. On either side of it, I put a strong steel trap. I kept my hands, boots, and tools smeared with fresh blood all the time. Afterward I dripped some blood all around on the ground.

When my traps were hidden in the dust, I brushed the place all over with the skin of a coyote. With the foot of the same coyote, I made tracks all around. I put the head of the cow beside a bush, leaving only a narrow space between. In the space I put two of my best traps, covered them with dust, and tied them to the head itself.

I knew that wolves will look over every body they get wind of, even if they do not want to eat it. I hoped that this habit would bring Lobo's pack within reach of my latest trick. I knew Lobo would know what I had done to the meat. But I hoped he would think the head had just been thrown away.

Next morning I could hardly wait to check my traps. I found the tracks of Lobo and his pack and followed them.

The beef head was gone. The traps were gone. I studied the tracks.

Lobo had kept his pack from going near the cow's body. But one wolf, a small one, had not obeyed him. It had gone on ahead to look at the head. This little wolf must have walked right into one of my hidden traps!

I set out on the trail. Within a mile I came upon the unlucky wolf. It was little Blanca. When she saw me, she tried to run away, trap and all. The head weighed more than fifty pounds, but she dragged it behind her. We would never have caught her if the cow's head hadn't caught in some rocks and held her fast.

What a beauty Blanca was! She was the finest wolf I had ever seen. Her coat was white and thick. She looked at us with hate in her yellow-green eyes. I got off my horse and started up into the rocks after her. She turned to fight me. She sent a long howl for help. I listened.

Sure enough, her answer came: the deep howl of Old Lobo.

15

The cowboy and I now closed in upon her. She needed all her strength and breath for the fight. The cowboy and I each threw a lasso over Blanca's neck. He pulled one way and I pulled the other. Her body went limp. We rode home with the dead Blanca.

All that day we could hear Lobo roar as he ran about looking for his mate. He could not save her, but he would not leave without her.

As evening fell, he seemed to come nearer. His voice was no longer a loud, angry howl. It was a long, sad wail.

"Blanca! Blanca!" he seemed to call, over and over again.

At last he found the spot where we had killed her. We could tell by his wail. The cowboys could not believe that an animal could sound so sad.

"I never heard an animal carry on like that before," one cowboy said. "Old Lobo seems to know just what happened to Blanca. He'll follow her here!"

At last Lobo took up our trail. He came closer to the ranch house. Did he hope to find Blanca alive? Or did he want to pay us back? We did not know.

That night he surprised our watchdog outside the gate and tore him to bits.

I began to wish I had not killed Blanca. If I had kept her alive, I might have got Lobo the next night. Now I got all the wolf traps I could find. I had one hundred thirty strong steel traps. I set them out, in groups of four, on every trail. Each trap was tied to a buried log. When the traps were all hidden, I dragged Blanca's body over each of them.

I also dragged it around the ranch. Then I cut off one of her paws and made a line of tracks over each trap. I used all the tricks I knew.

Once during the night I thought I heard Lobo, but I was not sure. Next day I rode to some of my traps. I found nothing.

"There was a lot of noise among the cattle this morning," a cowboy said at the supper table that night. "Maybe there is something in the traps near them."

It was late afternoon the next day before I got to the place. I saw a great, ugly form

on the ground, trying to escape. It was Lobo, caught in my traps. Poor old hero! He had never given up the search for his mate. When he had found her smell, he had followed it, and he had been caught in one set of my traps.

There he lay, the king of the Corrumpa, at the end of his trail. Four traps held him. He was helpless. He had lain there for two days and nights.

When I went near him, he stood up. His hair rose, and he howled for the last time. He called for help, but there was no answer. Lobo was alone in his pain. His life was almost gone, but he tried to get at me. Each trap was chained to a log that weighed over three hundred pounds. Each of his paws was caught in a trap. The heavy logs and the chains were all tangled together. He could not move.

How his long teeth dug into those chains! His eyes shone with hate and anger. His jaws snapped. He tried to reach me or my horse. But he was worn out from two days of fighting to get loose. Soon he sank to the ground.

"You grand old outlaw!" I said to him. "You are the hero of a thousand raids on the Corrumpa ranches. Soon you will be just a dead wolf. It can't be any other way!"

Then I swung my lasso and threw it over his head. But Lobo was far from dead. Before the rope fell on his neck, he grabbed it in his mouth and cut through it with one bite. The thick rope dropped in two parts at his feet.

I could have used my gun, but I did not want to spoil his hide. I jumped on my horse and rode back to camp. Soon I came back with new ropes and a cowboy to help me. The cowboy threw Lobo a stick of wood. Lobo grabbed it in his teeth. Before he could drop it, our ropes flew through the air. First one and then the other landed on his neck.

"Let's take him to camp alive," I said.

Lobo was helpless. We put a stick in his mouth, behind his teeth, and tied his jaws with a rope. Lobo stopped fighting and made no sound. He looked at us, as if to say, "Well, you have me at last. Do what you please with me."

From that time on, he did not look at us. Even when we tied him, he didn't growl or turn his head. He breathed evenly. His eyes were fixed on the faraway hills where his gray pack ran free. We went on slowly and at last reached the ranch. We staked him out in the grass. I put meat and water near him, but he didn't eat or drink. He lay on the ground, looking past me to the hills.

I thought he would call his band after it grew dark. We were ready for them. But he had called once. No one had come. He would never call again.

His strength gone, his freedom gone, his mate gone, Lobo lay looking toward the hills.

When morning came, he lay just as we had left him. His body was there, but his life was gone. The king of the wolves was dead!

PART 2

SILVERSPOT
the Story of a Crow

How many of us ever really get to know a wild animal? Even if we try to know one, we often have a hard time telling him from another. Unless he is very different, we cannot be sure that he is the same animal the next time we see him. But sometimes we find an animal who is a great leader. If he is bigger than the others, or has some mark by which we can spot him, he soon becomes well-known.

Silverspot, a wise old crow, was such a leader. He was given his name because of a silvery white spot as big as a nickel between his eye and his bill. Because he had this spot, I could tell him from other crows and learn his story.

Crows are very smart birds. They like to live together, and they depend on each other for help. A leader of crows must be the oldest, wisest, strongest, and bravest of the whole band.

Silverspot was the leader of about two hundred crows that lived in a pine forest in Canada. In mild winters these crows stayed in the north. During the colder winters, they flew south. I was new in Canada, but I soon saw the old crow and his band.

"That old crow has been flying around here for more than twenty years," an old-timer told me.

During the next few months, I saw Silverspot and his crows twice a day. I watched them fly back and forth over the valley. I heard Silverspot give orders to the others. And I saw the rest of the crows do what he told them. I soon learned what his calls meant. I learned to understand the crows' talk.

"Caw, caw," Silverspot would call to his band. This meant, "All's well. Come right along."

One day Silverspot saw me standing on a bridge, watching him.

"Caw!" he called, flying higher. This meant, "Be on your guard." When he saw I had no gun, he came down again.

On the third day, I took a gun with me. "Ca-ca-ca-ca-caw!" cried Silverspot. This meant, "Great danger—a gun!" The crows flew upwards, this way and that.

Another time Silverspot saw an enemy, a red-tailed hawk, waiting in a tree. "Caw!" he called, slowing up. All the other crows slowed up, too. They flew close together. In this way they were safer from attack.

The crows had many other signals which I learned to understand also.

Early in April the crows seemed to grow restless. They showed off their tricks of flying and made sounds I had not heard before. The crows were mating. By the middle of April they had gone all over the woods to build their nests.

One day I found Silverspot's nest. I was walking through the woods at dawn. The dead leaves on the ground were wet from the rain. They made no sound. I passed under an old hawk's nest in a tall pine. No one had seen a sign of life about this nest for many years. It was falling to pieces. But I saw a black tail sticking out of the nest.

I hit the tree with my walking stick. Off flew a large crow. It was Silverspot. The nest belonged to him and his mate. They had lived there for years, but they had never cleaned or fixed it. They had wanted everyone to think the nest was empty. This way they would be safe from the men and boys who hunted crows.

One day I saw Silverspot flying in the woods with something white in his mouth. He stopped on a hillside, and I watched him from behind a tree. He dug up a pile of shells and other white, shiny things. He laid them out in the sun, turned them over, and lifted them one by one in his beak. He played with them for about half an hour. Then he put dirt and leaves over them and flew away.

When he had gone, I went to the spot. I found white stones, clam shells, bits of tin, and the handle of a white cup. Later I went back again to see Silverspot's things, but they were gone. He knew that I had found them, so he had moved them. I never found the new hiding place.

Silverspot had many little adventures and escapes. Once I saw him beaten by a sparrow hawk. Another time I saw him chased by kingbirds. By watching him, I found that Silverspot himself had some tricks. Each morning, I found, he made his breakfast of the eggs of smaller birds.

Once I saw Silverspot drop some bread into a stream. It floated away under a bridge. Silverspot watched for a second. Then the smart old fellow flew to the other side of the bridge and waited. When the bread came by, he flew down and got it.

When the crows came together again at the end of June, they always made Silverspot their leader. At this time each year, the young crows of the band began their schooling. For the first week or two they made friends. After this, the older crows began to train the young ones. Each morning Silverspot made the young crows take orders. For the rest of the day they and the old crows looked all over the woods for food.

By fall the little crows knew how to drill. They knew about guns, traps, wireworms, and green corn. They knew that a young boy is to be feared more than a farmer's wife. They knew how to pick on a fox until he would give up half his dinner. Above all, they knew how to do what Silverspot wanted.

Silverspot became very happy. The young crows who had learned to obey him now learned to love him.

It was fun to watch Silverspot drill the young crows each morning.

"Fly!" he would call. A group of crows would fly forward.

"Up!" he would order. They would turn and fly upward.

"Together!" he would cry. They would fly together.

"Get away!" They would go this way and that like leaves in the wind.

"Get in line!" They would string out in a long line.

"Come down!" They would drop nearly to the ground.

"Eat!" They would come down and feed.

As I watched, I thought how much they were like soldiers learning to take orders.

There is only one time when a crow is a fool. That is at night. And there is only one bird that a crow fears. That is the owl. When an owl comes at night, the crows are afraid. But in the morning they grow braver, find him, and chase him from their woods.

The horned owl is the enemy the crows are most afraid of. One winter morning I found the track of a horned owl in the snow. Two days later, at dawn, there was a great noise among the crows. I went out early to see what had happened. I found some black feathers in the snow. A few feet away I saw the body of a crow. I could see that the crow had done his best, but that the horned owl had been too strong for him. I turned the body over. It was old Silverspot! His long life was ended. He had been killed by the owl that all the crows feared.

Silverspot's nest in the tall pine is empty now. The number of crows in the woods grows smaller every year. Without their wise leader, the band will soon be gone forever.

PART 3

RAGGYLUG
the Story of a Cottontail Rabbit

Raggylug was a young cottontail rabbit. He had a ragged ear which was torn on his first adventure. Raggylug lived with his mother in Olifant's Swamp. This is where I learned all the little things about his life that I put together to write this story.

RAGGYLUG'S FIRST ADVENTURE

Rabbits use sounds, signs, smells, whisker touches, and movements to talk to each other. It is not hard to understand rabbits.

Rag's mother had hidden him in a snug nest in the swamp. She had put grass over him to hide him.

"Lie low and say nothing, whatever happens!" she told him.

Raggylug lay still, but he was wide awake. He looked out into the trees above him.

31

He heard a bluejay and a red squirrel screaming at each other.

Just six inches from his nose, he saw a yellow songbird catch a blue butterfly. An orange-and-black ladybug walked across his face. But Raggylug didn't move. He didn't even wink.

After a while he heard a strange, new sound. It went on and on without stopping. It was not the pat of feet or the sound of wings. Rag had lived in the swamp all the three weeks of his life, but he had never heard a sound like it.

Raggylug wanted to know what that sound was. It came first from one side and then from the other. Then it seemed to be going away.

Raggylug felt that he just had to know what the noise was. He wasn't a baby, surely! He knew what he was doing.

Slowly he stood up and lifted his little round head over the top of his nest. He peeped out into the woods. The noise stopped. He took another step. He was face to face with a big black snake!

"Mommy!" he screamed.

The snake darted at Raggylug. With all the strength in his tiny legs, Rag tried to run. But the snake got him by one ear. It turned poor Rag around.

"Mommy! Mommy!" cried poor Raggylug, as the snake began slowly choking him to death.

Molly Cottontail ran through the swamp. She had heard Raggylug scream. She was no longer a shy, helpless, little bunny.

She hopped clear over the snake, hitting him with her strong hind feet as she went. She gave him a blow that made him twist with pain. He hissed angrily at her.

"Mommy!" Raggylug cried again.

She leaped again and again. Each time she hit the snake harder. At last the snake let go of Raggylug's ear and tried to get Molly as she jumped over him. But he could not reach her. Her hard kicks had torn bloody rips in the snake's hard skin.

Raggylug ran into the brush. He was out of wind and he shook with fear. Except for his torn left ear, he was not hurt.

As soon as Raggylug was safe, Molly also ran into the woods. Raggylug came after her to a safe part of the swamp.

OLD OLIFANT'S SWAMP

Old Olifant's Swamp was a wild piece of land. A little stream ran through the middle of it. There had been a forest fire some years before. Some of the old dead trees were still standing. Others were lying on the ground.

New trees were growing everywhere in the swamp. Cattails grew around the sides of the pond. Dry parts of the swamp were overgrown with brier bushes. All around the swamp was open land. The rabbits did not go out there into the open land.

The swamp was Molly's home and Rag's. There the two lived happily together. Molly was a good little mother. After he got away from the black snake, Rag did as his mother told him. He had learned his first lesson the hard way.

The second lesson he learned was to "freeze," or to sit without moving. As soon as a rabbit sees an enemy, he freezes. Since a rabbit is the same color as things in the woods, he can be seen only if he moves. If he freezes, he may save himself.

THE RABBIT'S BEST FRIEND

The best lesson that Rag learned from his mother was the brier-bush lesson. Why the brier bush fought with the animals is an old story. Here it is.

Long ago, roses grew on bushes that had no thorns. Squirrels and mice climbed after the roses. Cattle bumped them off with their horns. Possums hit them with their long tails. Deer broke them down with their feet. So the rose brier bush grew thorns and went to war with all animals that climbed trees or had horns, sharp feet, or long tails.

Since Molly Cottontail could not climb and had no horns or sharp feet but only a little tail, it and the rabbit stayed friends.

Since that time, whenever a bunny is in danger, he runs to the nearest rose brier bush. He knows that this good friend will help him with its sharp, poisoned thorns.

Molly Cottontail told this story to Raggy-lug. He learned that the rose brier bush is a rabbit's best friend.

During his first summer, Raggylug learned his way around the swamp. By the end of summer, he could go all around the swamp without leaving the friendly rose briers for more than five hops.

RAGGYLUG LEARNS A FEW TRICKS

Molly had no other children to look after now. She could give all of her time to Rag. He was a bright little rabbit. He was very strong. He got along well. Molly Cottontail showed Rag everything that she knew. He listened to her and did everything she did.

When she moved her nose "to keep her smeller clear," he did the same. He pulled food from her mouth or tasted her lips to make sure that he was getting the same kind of food. Rag learned to comb his ears with his claws. He learned to bite the burrs out of his coat. He learned to live in the swamp and the brier bush.

As soon as Rag was big enough to go out alone, Molly Cottontail showed him how to talk by thumping on the ground with his hind feet. Rabbits have keen ears, and they can hear thumps for a long way.

"Thump" means "Look out" or "Freeze." A slow "thump-thump" means "Come." A fast "thump-thump" means "Danger," and a very fast "thump-thump-thump" means "Run for your life."

Molly and Raggylug played hide-and-seek in the swamp. In this way Raggylug learned to find Molly easily and to follow a trail. Soon he knew about backtracking, log jumping, and many other tricks. He never forgot that "lie low" or "freeze" is the safest thing to do. He always remembered that the only safe place in a rabbit's world is the brier patch.

WARNINGS ABOUT A RABBIT'S ENEMIES

Raggylug's mother taught him to look out for hawks, owls, foxes, dogs, minks, weasels, cats, skunks, and men—all enemies of rabbits. Raggylug learned how to get away from all of them. He learned that he could get warning from his mother and the blue jay when danger was near.

Raggylug also learned to play a barbed-wire trick on dogs. The trick took much nerve. At first he was afraid. But when he learned how to play it, it was one of the games he liked best.

"First you lead a dog along," Molly told him. "Let him think he has almost got you. But stay out of his reach, just one hop ahead of him. Then lead him into a barbed-wire fence. I've seen many dogs and foxes hurt this way. I saw one big hound killed. But remember, a rabbit can also be hurt in a barbed-wire fence."

Raggylug learned when he was young not to run down into holes. By going down a hole, a rabbit may get away from the man, dog, fox, or owl that is chasing him. But he may run right down into the jaws of a mink, skunk, or weasel!

Raggylug and Molly Cottontail were the owners of two empty holes and a hollow tree. But they never went near any of them. They did not want to make a path that would lead the enemy to these hiding places.

A LESSON WITH OLIFANT'S DOG

It was a bright summer morning. The sun was warm in Olifant's Swamp. A brown swamp sparrow sat on a long weed in the pond. He saw two furry little animals hiding under a bush. He saw two little brown noses move up and down, up and down. Everything else in the swamp was still.

The sparrow was looking at Molly and Rag. They were stretched out under the leaves of a skunk cabbage. They did not like the bad smell of the skunk cabbage. But ticks didn't like it either, so here Rag and Molly were safe, even from ticks. They had come to this quiet place to rest and to enjoy the sun.

Suddenly they heard the blue jay's warning. Molly's ears went up. She raised her nose and got ready for any danger. Far across the swamp was Olifant's big black-and-white dog. He was looking for Molly and Rag!

"Freeze!" Molly ordered Raggylug. "I will go and keep that fool busy."

Away she went to meet the dog, running right across his path.

"Bow-ow-ow!" yelled the dog. He saw Molly and ran after her. Molly ran along in front of him. She led him to the brier patch. The thorns scratched him. They tore his ears and hurt his nose.

Then Molly ran through the briers. At last she led him into a barbed-wire fence. The dog gave up the chase. He went away howling with pain.

Molly came back over her own tracks. Then she made a loop. At last she came back to Rag. The little rabbit was standing up. He had been watching the chase.

Molly was angry. She had told him to lie still, but he had not done so. She hit him with her hind foot. Rag rolled over in the mud.

A LESSON WITH THE RED-TAILED HAWK

One day Molly and Rag were eating clover in Olifant's field. Suddenly a red-tailed hawk swooped down on them.

Molly kicked up her hind legs. She skipped away into the brier patch. The hawk could not follow.

They were in the main path through the briers. Several vines had grown across it. Keeping one eye on the hawk, Molly began to cut the vines off. Rag watched to see how she did it. Then he ran on ahead, helping her. He cut off vines across the path.

"That's right, Rag," said his mother. "Always keep your path clear. You will often need a clear path. It doesn't need to be wide, but it must be clear. Cut everything that looks like a vine."

"What looks like a vine, Mother?" asked Rag.

"A snare," Molly said.

"A snare? What is that?" Rag asked, scratching his ear with his hind foot.

"A snare looks like a vine, but it doesn't grow. It is worse than all the hawks in the world," said Molly. She looked up at the red-tailed hawk, which was now far away. "For the snare is in the path night and day. If it catches you, you can't get away."

"I don't believe a snare could catch me!" said Rag. He thought he was a big rabbit now. He rose on his heels and rubbed his chin and whiskers on a tree. Molly knew that when he did this he was no longer a baby. Rubbing his chin and whiskers on a tree was a sign that the little rabbit was growing up.

Molly was afraid for Rag. He was growing up, but he still had a lot more to learn.

THE LESSON OF RUNNING WATER

Running water can help animals. Every wild animal knows this. When the enemy is chasing him, he runs to the nearest running stream. He jumps into the water, splashes along in the stream for a while, and then runs back into the woods again. When the enemy comes to the stream, the water hides the trail, and he can no longer follow it. This was the next lesson that Molly taught Raggylug.

"After the brier patch, the water is your best friend," she told him over and over.

One hot night Molly led Rag through the woods. He followed her white tail in the dark. It was just like a lamp for him.

Soon they came to the pond. They stopped to listen.

"Sleep! Sleep!" sang the tree frogs all around them.

A bullfrog boomed on a sunken log out in the pond.

"Follow me!" said Molly. Rag watched.

With a splash Molly hopped into the pond. She swam toward the sunken log a few feet from the bank. Rag followed her into the water. He watched his mother closely and did everything she did. Through the water he went. He could swim!

When he came to the sunken log, Rag got up beside Molly on the high, dry end of the log. There was a screen of weeds around them.

"After this," Molly told him, "remember the water. Listen for the bullfrog's voice. He will tell you where the pond is. If you follow his voice and find the pond, you will be safe."

"What does the bullfrog say, Mother?"

"He says, 'Come when in danger! Come!'" answered his mother.

This was a good lesson for Raggylug. Many rabbits never live long enough to learn it.

RAGGYLUG GROWS UP

A rabbit is never safe. At least once a day Molly and Rag had to run for their lives. They saved themselves by their keen ears, their swift legs, and the lessons they had learned.

More than once that spring, the hated fox that lived in Olifant's Swamp chased Rag

43

and Molly. Once they got away from him by hiding under a roll of barbed wire near the spring. They watched the fox from their hiding place. The fox tore his legs on the barbed wire, but he could not reach them.

Raggylug got away from both a hound and a skunk at the same time. He got the hound to chase the skunk. And so Rag ran safely away.

Several times he got away from a hunter with a gun. Two or three times he was chased into the water by a cat. He was also chased by hawks and owls. But the older he grew, the wiser he became. The wiser he became, the better he was at saving himself.

RANGER THE HOUND

Ranger was the name of a young hound who lived near the swamp. Sometimes his master put him on Rag's trail. Rag enjoyed the chase as much as the hound did.

"Oh, Mother," Rag would say, "here comes the hound again. Today we can have another chase!"

"You are too bold, Raggy," Molly would tell him. "You will run once too often!"

"But, Mother," he would tell her, "it is such fun to tease the hound. And it's good training for me. I'll thump if I get into danger. Then you can come to help me. We can change off till I get my breath again."

Ranger would follow Raggylug's trail. When Rag got tired of the chase, he would thump for help. Then Molly would come. She would get the dog to see her. Then they would be off on another chase while Rag rested. Sometimes Rag would get rid of Ranger by using one of the many tricks he knew.

HOW RAG FOOLED RANGER

Here is the story of one chase that will show you how well Raggylug had learned all the tricks of the woods.

Rag knew that the dogs could smell him best when he ran on the ground. He knew if he could get off the ground for a while, he could rest. In this time his trail would cool off. A cool trail would be hard for the hound to follow. Then Rag would be safe.

So when Rag grew tired of the chase, he ran to the brier patch. He turned left and

right and crossed his own trail. The hound slowed up, trying to find out which way he had gone.

Then Rag jumped onto a log. He ran to the higher end of the log and sat without moving.

By the time Ranger again found Rag's trail, it was cold. At last he passed right under the log where Rag was sitting. Rag sat very still. He never moved. He never even winked. The hound passed by. He nosed along the other end of the log. He stopped to sniff. The rabbit smell was weak, but he knew Rag had been there.

It was a bad time for Rag. Ranger sniffed along the log, just a few feet away. Rag planned to run when Ranger came halfway. But Ranger didn't come that close. He didn't look up and see the rabbit. The trail ran out, and Ranger left the log. Raggylug had fooled Ranger again. He was safe.

A STRANGE RABBIT COMES TO THE SWAMP

Rag had never seen a rabbit other than his mother. He had never even asked if there were any other rabbits in the world.

47

One day in winter he saw a strange rabbit in the swamp. Raggylug watched the stranger. He hated him as soon as he saw him.

The strange rabbit stopped at one of Rag's rubbing trees. He rubbed his chin as far up as he could reach on the tree. All buck rabbits have rubbing trees. Rubbing on a tree tells others rabbits that the tree already belongs to someone. It means "Stay away."

Rag saw that the strange rabbit was a head taller than he was. He was angry. He hopped ahead to the hard ground. Then he thumped slowly and loudly.

"Thump! Thump! Thump!"

This meant, "Get out of my swamp or fight!"

The strange rabbit made a big v with his ears. He sat up high for a few seconds. Then he dropped to his forefeet. With his hind feet he thumped back.

"Thump! Thump! Thump!"

And so the war was on.

The stranger was a big heavy buck. He had big strong legs. He soon showed that he was not smart. But he was very strong.

The stranger ran at Rag. Rag met him. Both rabbits jumped up, turned, and kicked out with their hind feet.

Thud! Thud! Down went poor little Rag.

In a flash, the stranger was on him, biting him with sharp teeth. Rag jumped away. The stranger got him down and bit him many times.

Rag knew he must run for his life. He ran away. The stranger followed.

Rag was a good runner. The big, heavy stranger soon gave up the chase. He was stiff and sore.

Molly had showed Rag how to get away from all his other enemies. But Molly had never told him how to get away from another rabbit. He could only hide and run.

Molly did not know how to help Rag.

The big buck found her, too. When she tried to run away from him, he caught her. He followed her. He pushed her down. He tore out her soft fur.

Whenever Rag took a nap, he had to be ready to run. Many times each day the stranger came up while Rag slept. Each time Rag woke up in time to save his life. But what a life it had become! Rag hated the stranger more than he had ever hated another enemy. How was it all to end?

Things got worse. Rag was always tired. The stranger was trying his best to kill Rag. At last the stranger did the most terrible thing a rabbit can do.

No matter how much they hate each other, rabbits always help one another when a hawk comes. One day a big hawk flew over Olifant's Swamp. What did the stranger do? He stayed under cover and tried to drive Rag into the open. Rag had to run from both the hawk and the stranger. Only the briers saved him.

RAG WINS

Rag knew that he and Molly would have to leave Olifant's Swamp. They would have to give up their home to the stranger. They would have to find a new place to live.

But one day Rag heard Ranger, the hound. Ranger was sniffing around Olifant's Swamp.

Rag came out of his hiding place. He hopped in front of Ranger. The chase was on.

They raced three times around the swamp. Rag knew that his mother was hidden in a safe place. He also knew the stranger was in his nest. What do you think Rag did? He jumped right into the stranger's nest, kicked him, and ran on.

The stranger jumped. He chased Rag. But he found himself between Rag and the hound. What a spot he was in!

The stranger could not run very fast. He did not know many tricks. The quickest runner would win the race. Raggylug hopped away. He and Molly listened to the noise of the chase. Suddenly it stopped. They heard a loud scream. Rag and Molly knew that the swamp was theirs again.

THE WINTER PASSES

Mr. Olifant was a farmer. In the winter he burned all the brush and took away the roll of barbed wire just below the spring. Every farmer does these clean-up jobs.

But it was hard on Rag and Molly to lose some of their hiding places. They had been in Olifant's Swamp for a long time. They felt that they owned it.

During a warm spell in January, Mr. Olifant cut down trees around the pond for firewood. This, too, was very hard on the rabbits. They lost some good hiding places.

When the snow was almost all gone and the days were bright and warm, Molly went to find teaberries. Rag sat and warmed himself in the sun.

In the farmyard Olifant was feeding his animals cabbage. The horses, cows, and sheep ate the green leaves. Rag's mouth watered. He loved cabbage. But he remembered that he had been to the barnyard only the night before for clover. No wise rabbit goes to the same place two nights in a row.

So Rag did a wise thing. He hopped away until he could not smell the cabbage. He made his supper of some hay. Later on, Molly joined him for the night. She had eaten her teaberry leaves. For supper she had eaten sweet birchbark.

It was a bitter cold night. It was worse than when the ground was covered with snow, for the snow made many warm hiding places.

"What a bitter cold night!" said Raggy-lug. "I wish we had a warm brush pile!"

"It would be good to sleep in the hole under the pine tree," said Molly. "But we have not seen that mink's hide nailed up on the barn door yet. Until we do, it's not safe to go into any hole."

The hollow hickory tree was gone, too. It was in Olifant's wood lot. In it was the mink they feared. Molly and Rag would have been safe in the hole under the pine tree. But they did not know it.

They hopped off to the south side of the pond. They went under a pile of brush. There they stayed for the night. They sat down back to back. They were on guard, even when they were asleep.

The wind blew harder and harder as the night went on. Soon an icy snow began to fall.

The old fox was hungry. He was out hunting. He came upon Molly and Rag. The noise of the wind and the snow helped him to get near before Molly heard him. The faint sound of a dry leaf under the fox's paw woke her.

Molly woke Rag. Just as the fox sprang on them, Molly jumped out into the storm. The fox went after her. Rag jumped to one side.

Molly raced for her life. She came to the pond and jumped into the deep water. The fox swam right after Molly. But the water was too cold for him. He turned back for the other shore.

The icy waves broke over Molly's head as she swam. The water was bitter cold and full of snow and ice. The other shore seemed very far away.

Molly had nearly reached the other shore when some snow slid down from the bank. It pushed her back into the icy pond.

Again she swam for the shore. When at last she reached the bank, her legs were stiff from cold. Her strength was almost gone. Her brave little heart was sinking. She didn't care whether the fox was waiting for her or not. She pulled her little body into the reeds. But once in the reeds, her strokes stopped. She could swim no more. In a little while she stopped moving. Her soft brown eyes closed in death.

The fox was no longer waiting for Molly Cottontail. Even Rag didn't know that. He had run back to help Molly. He had planned to change off with her and wear out the fox so that both of them would get away.

He met the fox just after Molly jumped into the pond. The fox set off after Raggylug. They raced for the barbed wire. The fox was badly cut and gave up.

Then Raggylug looked for his mother. He thumped and thumped. But he got no answer. He could not find his mother. He never saw her again. He never knew what happened to her.

Poor little Molly Cottontail! She had made a good fight all her life. And she lives on in Raggylug.

WHAT HAPPENED TO RAGGYLUG

Rag still lives in Olifant's Swamp. Old Olifant died that winter. His lazy sons did no more work clearing the swamp. They fixed no more fences. They cut no more firewood.

They moved away from the farm. The brush and briers grew thicker. The fences fell down, and the barbed wires became real death traps for foxes and hounds. In a year it was a wild place, and a better place for rabbits.

Raggylug lives in the swamp to this day. He is a big strong buck. He has a pretty brown wife—I don't know where he got her —and a large family of his own.

There, at Olifant's Swamp, Rag's family will live forever. You may see them there any time. If you know just how and when to thump in rabbit talk, you will soon have an answer!

PART 4

*W*ULLY
the Story of a Yellow Dog

Wully was a little yellow dog. This does not just mean that his coat was yellow in color. It means that he was a real cur. Many different kinds of dogs were mixed up in him.

Such a yellow dog does not have the speed of a greyhound. He is not so strong as a bulldog. But, like the wild dogs, he has something much better. He has common sense. Wully was such a dog. He had many good things about him. He also had a wild streak in him.

Wully was born in the northern part of England, in sheep-raising country. He was trained as a sheep dog by an old shepherd named Robin. Robin was a lazy, stupid man. Wully was a bright little dog. But Robin was not cruel to him, and Wully loved the foolish old man. By the time Wully was two years

old, Robin knew he could trust the dog to do his work for him. Wully knew so much about the sheep that Robin often stayed all night in town.

One summer Robin was told to drive his 374 sheep to market. During the first part of the trip, Wully kept the sheep together. They moved quietly along. But after they crossed a big river on a ferry boat, they came to a town where there were many factories. The town was noisy, smoky, and dirty. The sheep were scared. They thought a storm was coming. They ran off this way and that way.

Robin just looked at the running sheep. He did not know what to do. "Wully," he said, "get them in." Then the old man lit his pipe and sat down on a rock to wait.

Wully knew just what to do. It was not an easy job, but before too long the yellow dog had chased all the sheep back.

Robin counted the sheep. ". . . 370, 371, 372, 373. They're not all here, Wully," he said.

Wully felt ashamed. Up and down the city streets he ran, looking for the lost sheep. He had not been gone long when a small boy came by.

"What are you waiting for, old man?" he asked.

"I should have 374 sheep," Robin said, "but I have only 373. I am waiting for my dog to find the missing one."

"Maybe you counted wrong," said the boy. He began to count, ". . . 372, 373, 374. They're all here," he said. "You did count wrong."

Robin was in a hurry to get his sheep to market. He knew Wully would be gone for a long time. So he did not wait for the little dog, but went on.

Poor Wully looked for the missing sheep all day long. When he came back to the ferry boat that night, he was tired and very hungry. He looked for Robin and the flock. He rode back and forth on the ferry boat. He cried. On the next day he began to smell everybody that crossed the river on the boat.

The ferry made fifty trips across the river each day. About one hundred people went across on every trip. Wully sniffed five thousand pairs of legs each day, week after week. He became cross. He was hungry. He let no one touch him. At last he ate the food the ferry boatmen put out for him. But he would not make friends with any of them. He was true to Robin, his master.

Day after day, week after week, Wully waited for his master. Wully was sure that Robin wanted him to stay by the ferry. And stay he did, for two long years. The ferry captain said that Wully had sniffed at least six million pairs of legs. Robin never came.

WULLY FINDS A NEW MASTER

One day a shepherd got on the boat. Wully ran to him, wagged his tail, and tried to lick the shepherd's hands. The man, Dorley, had known Robin. He wore mittens and a scarf of Robin's, which Robin had given him. Wully knew his master's clothing. He felt happy. He stayed with Dorley. Dorley was happy to have the dog. He took Wully home and had him take care of his flock of sheep. Once more, Wully was a sheep dog.

Wully watched over Dorley's sheep so well that Dorley did not lose one lamb in a whole year. But Wully had become a very mean dog. He growled at everyone and was always ready to show his teeth. Dorley and his daughter Huldah were the only ones who could touch the yellow dog.

That year a fox came to live near Dorley's place. He killed sheep and chickens. He was so sly that the dogs could not catch him. He always got away by running to the Devil's Hole, a rocky place where he could not be followed. The farmers called him the Devil's Fox.

Soon the fox began to kill just for the sake of killing. He killed lambs, ducks, sheep, chickens, and finally he even killed cows. No one ever got a good look at him. But they could tell from his tracks that he was a very big fox.

The farmers got together to get rid of the fox in any way they could. They knew that if it should snow, they could follow his tracks until they found him.

The fox was smart. He never came to the same farm two nights in a row. He never ate in the same place he killed. And he never left a trail. He went home on the big road, so he could not be trailed.

Only Dorley was not robbed by the fox. This was very strange, for Dorley lived only a mile from Devil's Hole.

Wully was a better sheep dog than any other dog around. Night after night he came in with the sheep. Not one was ever missing. But Wully's temper got worse and worse. He would have nothing to do with anyone but Dorley and Huldah. He often tried to bite people. He was even mean to other dogs.

Yet Wully was always gentle with Dorley's sheep and lambs. He helped them out of trouble. Everyone knew what a good sheep dog Wully was.

TRACKING THE DEVIL FOX

The fox was still killing sheep when, late in winter, the snow came. The farmers took their guns and set out to track down the killer. They followed his trail to the river. The sly fox had jumped into the water. The farmers looked up and down the banks for a long time. At last they found the spot where the fox had come out of the water.

Then they followed the trail to a high stone wall. They lost the trail at one place and found it again going into a farm. The Devil Fox had walked in the footprints of a man for a little way and then had gone along the road. His tracks went right to Dorley's farm.

Dorley had kept the sheep in the barn that day because of the snow. Wully was lying in the sun. When he saw the hunters, he growled and went to be with the sheep. One of the farmers looked at Wully's tracks in the snow.

"Men," he said, "we're not following a fox. There's the killer!" Some of the other men agreed with him. They thought Wully was the killer. Dorley heard them talking and came out of his house.

"Dorley," said one farmer, "your dog killed twenty of Widow Gelt's sheep last night. And I, for one, don't think it was his first killing!"

"Why, man, you must be wrong," said Dorley. "I've never had a better sheep dog. Wully loves the sheep."

The farmers told Dorley what they had found that morning. But Dorley thought they were just trying to get Wully away from him.

"Wully sleeps in the kitchen every night," he told them. "He's never out but when he's with the sheep. And I haven't lost one all year."

HULDAH'S PLAN

The men did not know what to do. But Huldah had a good plan. "Father," she said, "let me sleep in the kitchen tonight. If Wully leaves, I'll see him. And if he's not out and sheep are killed, we'll know that he's not the killer."

That night Huldah slept in the kitchen. Wully slept in his place under the table. Late in the night, Wully got restless. He turned about. He got up, stretched, looked at the sleeping girl, and lay down again. Then he rose softly. Huldah lay still. Her breathing was steady. Wully came near and sniffed her face. He poked at her with his nose. Then Wully walked quietly to the window, raised it with his nose, jumped out, and ran off.

Huldah was not asleep. She watched Wully. She started to call her father, but then waited until she was more sure that Wully was the killer. She put wood on the fire and lay down again. Then she waited for him to come back. Three hours later, Wully came in through the window and closed it behind him.

THE DEVIL FOX IS CAUGHT

In the light of the fire, Huldah saw that Wully's eyes shone wildly. She saw that his jaws and chest were full of blood! The dog looked over at her. When she did not move, he lay down and began to lick himself clean.

Huldah had seen enough. She sat up. "So it's true," she cried. "Oh, Wully, you brute!"

Wully jumped up. His fur rose. But he crawled over to her as if he wanted to lick her feet. He seemed to beg her to forgive him. Closer and closer he crawled. Suddenly, without a sound, he jumped for her throat.

Huldah was taken by surprise. She threw up her arm. Wully's long sharp teeth cut her to the bone. "Help! Help!" she screamed.

She was able to push Wully away, but he came back again. He knew it was her life or his.

"Father!" she cried. "Father! Help!"

Wully bit and tore at her hands, the hands that had fed him. He almost had her by the throat when Dorley rushed into the kitchen. Wully sprang at the farmer, too, and tore his arm. But Dorley had brought a heavy club with him. With it he hit the yellow dog. Wully fell to the floor. Dorley hit him again. The second blow killed him. There, with the friends who had trusted him, Wully—sheep dog by day, sheep killer by night—shook for a moment, then lay forever still.

PART 5

RED RUFF
the Story of a Partridge

Down the hill Mother Partridge led her babies. Her little ones were only one day old. They were going to the brook to drink for the first time. Mother Partridge walked slowly, for the woods were full of enemies. She clucked softly, calling to the twelve little partridges who followed her.

The babies were not much larger than acorns. They were covered with soft down. If one of them was left even an inch behind, he cried.

Mother Partridge watched each of them. She also watched the bushes, the trees, and the sky, for partridges have many enemies and few friends. Suddenly she saw the fox coming toward them over the hill. There was no time to lose.

"Hide! Hide!" she cried. The tiny birds ran to hide. One went under a leaf. Another sat between two roots. A third crawled into a bit of bark. A fourth hid in a hole. All but one of the babies found a place to hide. At last this one sat on a broad yellow chip of wood. He closed his eyes tightly and sat very still.

Mother Partridge flew right at the fox. She dropped to the ground near him. She flopped about as if hurt and lame, and cried. Was she begging the fox to let her go? She was no fool. Wait and see what a fool she made of the fox!

"Ah," thought the fox, "a fine partridge. And she's right within my reach!" The fox turned quickly and just missed catching Mother Partridge. She flopped away again. He jumped at her. She flopped behind a small tree and dragged herself under a log. The fox snapped. He almost had her that time! He jumped over the log, hoping to catch her on the other side. But Mother Partridge went on down a dusty bank.

The fox was right behind her. He almost caught her tail. But something was very strange. No matter how fast he went, Mother

Partridge always went a little faster. She seemed to get stronger. When they were far away from the place where she had left her babies, she flapped her wings, rose into the air, and flew off into the woods. The fox was left behind. This was not the first time Mother Partridge had fooled him. But he never found out that this was the way she kept enemies away from her family.

Mother Partridge flew over the woods and back to her babies. They were just where she had left them. Not one of them had moved.

"Come, children," she said. The little fellow on the wood chip opened his eyes. All twelve babies ran to their mother, and she clucked to them.

Now the sun was hot. The partridge family had to cross an open space to get to the brook. Mother Partridge looked carefully about for enemies. Then she spread her tail and got her children under it. When they reached the brier patch by the stream, a cottontail rabbit jumped out ahead of them. He was an old friend, and he meant no harm to the partridge family.

At first the babies did not know how to drink. By watching their mother and doing what she did, they soon learned. When they had drunk, Mother Partridge led them to an ants' nest. She stepped on top of it and broke it open with her sharp claws. The ants crawled out into the sunshine. Some of them carried fat white eggs. Mother Partridge picked up one of these eggs in her beak. She clucked and dropped it. Then she picked it up again and ate it. The little ones stood around, watching their mother. Then the baby who had sat on the chip picked up an egg, dropped it, picked it up again, and ate it. He had learned to eat. Within twenty minutes all his brothers and sisters had also learned to eat. They ate the ant eggs until they were full.

Next Mother Partridge led them to a sandy bank where they had a nap all afternoon. They scratched, rolled in the dust, and flopped their tiny wings. How good they felt!

That night Mother Partridge took them to some bushes nearby. The twelve tired babies got close to her. Soon they were asleep.

A WEEK GOES BY

By the third day the chicks were stronger. They were growing fast. They could climb right over an acorn. They could climb over a pine cone. Blue feathers began to grow on their wings. A week later they had learned to fly.

The twelve babies needed a good mother. They also needed good legs. Most of all, they needed good sense.

All the babies were soon strong on the wing, but one little brother was unlucky. The day before, the mother had seen a skunk nearby.

"Fly! Fly!" she had called.

Away they flew. But this little fellow wasn't fast enough. When the mother counted her family under the pine tree, one was missing. They saw him no more.

NOW THERE ARE ELEVEN

The little partridges learned to find the best grasshoppers. They learned where to find smooth green worms. They went to the ant hills for fat white eggs.

They loved to eat wild strawberries and

butterflies. They also ate many kinds of bugs. But they did not eat hornets, wasps, wooly worms, or worms with many legs.

By July, the partridges had grown larger. Their mother could no longer cover them with her wings. The family had new adventures every day.

They had found a new place to take their daily dust bath. It was higher on the hill. Many other birds used it. At first, Mother Partridge did not like the idea of a second-hand bath. But her children loved to go there, so she forgot her fears.

SICKNESS COMES TO THE PARTRIDGE FAMILY

Before long, all the partridges grew sick. Mother Partridge did not know that the new dust bath was full of worms. The worms had gone inside the birds. Mother Partridge looked for a cure for her sickness.

Finally she found some poison sumac berries. She did not like the bitter berries, but she ate them anyway. She and her children ate and ate.

No doctor could have found a better cure. The poison berries killed the worms inside the partridge family. But the cure came too late for four of the little partridges.

The same skunk that had captured the other little partridge found the four dead brothers lying by the stream. He ate their bodies, but the poison they had eaten killed him.

AND NOW THERE ARE SEVEN

Of the seven little partridges who were left, Mother Partridge liked the biggest one best. He was the one who had hidden on the chip. He had been first to learn to eat. He was not only the largest of the family, he was also the strongest and the best-looking partridge. Best of all, he did what he was told. Because of this, he lived the longest.

Summer passed. Now the young ones were almost grown. They thought they were very wise. At this time of year weasels, foxes, skunks, and mink were all around. The nights were dangerous for the partridge family. Mother Partridge showed her children how to sleep in the trees.

But one little partridge would not obey. He liked to sleep on the ground, and he would not change. During the night they heard him cry out. There was a little noise, then all was still.

Mother Partridge looked out into the darkness. She saw two close-set eyes shining below. She knew that a mink had killed her child.

NOW THERE ARE SIX

Six little partridges now sat in a row at night. Their mother sat in the middle. If one was cold, he would climb onto his mother's back.

Each day they learned new lessons. About this time Mother Partridge showed them how to whirr.

Whirring is a way to give warning. It tells other partridges that danger is near. It surprises the hunter. Sometimes one partridge will whirr while the others get away. Sometimes they will all fly softly away. Sometimes they will sit quietly and never be seen.

For partridge, every month of the year brings new enemies. It also brings new kinds of food. A partridge has different things to learn every month.

In fall when the berries were gone, the partridges ate seeds and grain. And now there were hunters.

The partridges knew what a fox was. They knew they could get away from a fox by flying into a tree. But one day a hunter came with a dog.

"Fly away!" cried Mother Partridge, rising on silent wings.

All but two of her children followed her. These two thought their mother was foolish to fly away. Thinking the dog was a fox, they flew into a tree.

The barking dog ran to the tree. The two partridges did not see the hunter creeping nearer and nearer in the tall grass.

Bang! Bang! Down fell two bloody partridges. The dog grabbed them and carried them to the hunter.

NOW THERE ARE FOUR

The hunting season starts on a special day each fall. This hunter was out ahead of time.

For the rest of that month, the partridges kept out of his way. They also kept away from their old enemies. The leaves had not yet fallen, so they hid in the trees.

When the leaves fell and the nights grew colder, the owls came from the north. The partridges moved to the thickest part of an evergreen tree.

Only one of the little family would not move. He stuck to the swinging branch of the elm tree. He was too sleepy to move. Before morning, an owl had carried him off.

NOW THERE ARE THREE

The three young partridges that were left were now as big as their mother. One was even bigger than his mother. Remember the little fellow on the chip, the one that learned to eat first? Well, he was now bigger than his mother.

The tips of the young partridges' ruffs were beginning to show. They were all proud of their new ruffs, for a ruff is a sign of growing up. A partridge hen has a black ruff with light green shine. The ruff of the male partridge is much larger than a hen's. It is blacker, too. It has a brighter green shine.

Sometimes there is a very large male partridge whose large ruff is colored red, gold, green, and purple. He is a beautiful bird.

The little fellow who had hidden on the chip was such a partridge. He was the handsomest partridge that had ever been seen in all that country. People called him Red Ruff.

It was a warm day in fall. The partridge family was sitting in the sun near a fallen pine. Suddenly Red Ruff jumped upon the log. He marched up and down, whirred his wings loudly, and then drummed on the log. He had never done this before, but he enjoyed it.

His brother and sister thought he had done a fine thing! They were very proud of him. But from that time on, his mother was a little afraid of him. She knew that Red Ruff was now all grown-up.

THE MAD MOON

The November moon is called the Mad Moon. All partridges go crazy in November of their first year. Even the wisest partridges will do foolish things at this time. Some race around the country at night. Sometimes they fly into wires. Sometimes they dash into buildings. Sometimes they fly into trains.

When morning comes, they are found in many strange places.

November madness does one good thing: it breaks up partridge families so that brothers and sisters cannot mate. Sometimes madness comes again in the second November. But it never comes in the third.

The wild grapes ripened, and the maple leaves turned red and gold. One day a flock of wild geese honked overhead. They were going south. The young partridges thought they were long-necked hawks. They were afraid. But they saw that their mother was not afraid, so they watched the flock of geese.

The November moon grew larger. When it was full, November madness came. The little family broke up. Red Ruff himself took several long, crazy, night trips. He was gone for a few days. When he came back, he found himself alone.

WINTER COMES

Soon it was winter. The ground was covered with snow. Red Ruff ate winter berries. He broke through the ice to get food. Sharp, horny points grew on his feet, making them like snowshoes for walking on ice and snow.

Red Ruff grew wiser and more beautiful every day. The snow made it easier to see his enemies. Most of the hawks and owls had flown away.

Nor were there other partridges about. Red Ruff did not know where they had gone, but he did not miss them. In time he found great banks of wintergreen berries. Then he did not have to work so hard for his food. His worn beak began to grow out again. The snow began to melt.

AND NOW IT IS SPRING

When the first bluebird came, Red Ruff knew that spring was on its way. Soon Old Silverspot, the king of the crows, flew from the south, followed by his flock.

"Caw, caw!" shouted Silverspot. "Spring has come!"

All the birds went wild that spring. They sang so much they barely had time to eat. The world was full of birds' song.

Red Ruff also felt happy that spring had come. Now he jumped upon a stump. He thumped and drummed with all his might.

The sound of his drumming rolled down the valley. He showed the world how glad he was that it was spring.

Not far off, the hunter heard Red Ruff drumming.

"I hear a partridge!" he said to his wife. "I think I'll get him!"

But Red Ruff flew silently away. He found another log in a safe spot. Again and again he drummed. He was like a little boy who had just learned a new trick.

A schoolboy heard Red Ruff drumming. He ran home as fast as his legs would carry him.

"Mother," he yelled, "the Indians are on the warpath. I heard them!"

"That is only a partridge," his mother laughed. "He is feeling happy today."

RED RUFF DRUMS

Red Ruff was feeling happy indeed. He drummed and marched. He was proud of his beautiful colored ruff shining in the sun. He drummed in his drumming place day after day. Now he had two rose-red combs, one above each eye. His big snowshoes were gone.

He was very beautiful. He was also very lonesome.

He didn't know what to do but keep on drumming. One day he heard a soft footstep in the woods. He stood very still and watched.

Was someone there? Yes! It was a shy little partridge hen. She was looking for a place to hide!

In a moment, Red Ruff was beside her. He opened his fine feathers! His ruff caught golden lights from the sun. He marched before her. He turned himself every way. He clucked softly to her. He thought her heart was nearly won.

Nearly won! Her heart had been won three days before. She had come at his first drumming on the log. She had been watching him ever since. Why had he not found her sooner?

Many happy days followed. The spring sun was never brighter. The spring air was never softer. The birds' songs were never sweeter. Red Ruff drummed for the joy of being alive.

Red Ruff's little brown mate sometimes slipped away. She stayed with him less and less. Then she did not come to him at all.

Red Ruff drummed on his old log. Then he flew upstream to another log. He drummed and he drummed. Then he went back to the log where he had first found the little hen. He drummed again.

RED RUFF'S FAMILY

He heard a sound in the bushes. There was the little brown hen. Ten little peeping partridges followed her. Red Ruff went to her side. When they saw him, the babies ran to their mother. Red Ruff watched her cover the little ones with her wings. Then Red Ruff joined the family. From that day on he helped care for the babies.

Good partridge fathers are few and hard to find. The mother often builds her nest alone. She hatches her young and raises them without help. She even hides the nest from the father. She meets him at the drumming place or at the dusting place, alone.

Red Ruff helped teach the babies to eat and drink. He taught them things that he had learned long ago. The mother led the way. The little ones followed her. Last of all came Red Ruff.

One day as they walked along, a red squirrel peeped around the trunk of a pine tree. He watched them. He saw the smallest one coming last. This seemed a good chance for him to taste a fat little partridge. He did not see Red Ruff, who walked a few yards behind them all.

The squirrel ran at the little partridge. Red Ruff saw him. He flew right into the squirrel, thumped the squirrel with his feet, and beat him with his wings. What a blow he could strike! He hit the squirrel right on the nose and knocked him into a brush pile.

The family went on toward the brook. A cow had left deep tracks in the sand. A little partridge fell into one. He peeped loudly. Red Ruff did not know what to do. Neither did the hen. They tramped around the track. They broke the side of the little hole, and so the little one walked out. He ran to his brothers under the broad fan of his mother's tail.

Red Ruff was proud of his family. He was always with them. He always watched over them.

In June a boy with a dog came by. The dog was running on ahead. Red Ruff ran to meet the dog. He tried his mother's old trick, acting as if he were hurt. He led the dog away from his little partridge family. Then Red Ruff rose on silent wings and flew back to his babies.

The little brown partridge cried, "Hide! Hide!"

Then she ran out to meet the boy. She hopped out of the grass, then rolled over into the leaves. She seemed to be lame. For a while the boy was fooled.

Next she dragged one wing, cried, and crawled away. The boy tried to hit her with a stick. He missed. She limped behind a small tree. She beat her wings upon the ground. The boy tried to hit her again.

He missed again. She moaned, as if begging for help. Then the boy raised his gun. He shot the little mother into bloody rags.

The boy looked all around for baby partridges. Not one of them moved or peeped. He tramped all around. More than one of the silent little partridges were crushed under his feet.

Red Ruff now had led the dog far away. When he got back, the boy had gone. He had thrown the hen's body away. Red Ruff looked around. He found the bloody spot and some feathers.

How can I tell you how Red Ruff felt? Then he thought of his poor, motherless babies. Back to their hiding place he flew.

"Kreet! Kreet!" he called.

Did every hiding place give up its little bird? No. Six little babies came running to meet him. Four little ones were dead. Red Ruff called again and again. At last he knew that the other four would not come. Then he led his six babies far away to a place where the barbed wire and brier bushes were thick. This would be a better home for his family.

ANOTHER FAMILY GROWS UP

Here the partridge family grew up. Red Ruff trained them, just as his mother had trained him. The summer passed, and not another partridge was lost.

Red Ruff had stopped drumming after his

mate was killed. But in September he again stood on a log and drummed. Some of the young ones tried it, too. Soon the males were all drumming.

The Mad Moon came again. Red Ruff's family got the madness, but only three of them flew away for good. Three stayed. Red Ruff and these three were still living in the same place when the first snow came. The snow piled up, and the air was bitter cold.

Red Ruff showed the others a good trick. He found a deep pile of snow and dived into it. The others followed him. Wind blew loose snow into the holes and covered them. There they slept.

The next night they slept in the snow again. During the night the wind changed. Sleet and rain fell. The snow was coated with ice, and the partridges were caught inside.

Red Ruff made his way to the top. But he could not get through the ice. He hammered and pushed. He hurt his head and wings. He grew weaker all the time. He heard his hungry family calling to him for help, but he could not help them.

When night fell, the partridges grew quiet. They had almost given up. At first Red Ruff was afraid the fox would come by and dig them out. By the second night he even wished that the fox would come. If the fox broke the ice, they would have a chance!

Then the fox did come. But the partridges kept still until he passed on. The second day another snow fell. By the third day the ice seemed thinner. Red Ruff picked it with his beak.

At last, just before the sun went down, he broke through. He pushed his head through, then his broad shoulders, and then his beautiful ruff. In a little while, Red Ruff jumped out of the snowy bed that had almost been his grave!

First he flew to the nearest berry bush. He was almost dead of hunger, and he needed food. Then he went back to the snowbank. He clucked and stamped, trying to find his family.

"Peet, peet!" he heard.

Scratching with his sharp claws on the thin ice, Red Ruff soon broke through. Gray

Tail crawled out of the drift. But the others gave no sign of life. He had to leave them.

It took Red Ruff and Gray Tail a long time to get strong. They ate winter berries and rested. By midwinter they were well and strong.

Again a hunter came. He was looking for partridge. He had heard about the beautiful Red Ruff. He was looking for Red Ruff. He came day after day. Red Ruff knew good hiding places. He knew good tricks. He knew when to rise on his big silent wings.

Red Ruff moved to another part of the country. It was a good feeding ground. All kinds of fine berries grew there. Acorns could be found under the snow. If a hunter came, there would be many hiding places.

The hunter found Red Ruff's hiding place. This time the hunter had a friend to help him. The hunter went under the bank. The friend sent his hound around to drive the partridges. Then he came tramping through the bushes.

"R-r-r-r!" warned Red Ruff, walking quickly toward a pine tree.

Gray Tail was farther up the hill. She saw the hound. She knew that Red Ruff could not see the dog.

"Kwit! Kwit!" cried Gray Tail.

"Fly! This way! Hide!" Red Ruff warned.

Then Red Ruff heard a noise under the bank. He knew it was an enemy. Gray Tail cried out as the dog jumped at her. She rose in the air, flying behind the tree, away from the hunter she could see. But she went right over the second hunter under the bank.

He fired his gun. Down she fell, wounded and bleeding. She died in the snow.

It was a dangerous place for Red Ruff. He got down low. The dog came within ten feet of him. The hunter came within five feet of him. He didn't move. At last he slipped behind the tree. He got away from both dog and man, and flew away on silent wings.

One by one, Red Ruff's loved ones had been killed. Now he was alone. Winter passed. Red Ruff had many more adventures. He was the only partridge of his kind left. He was always chased. He grew wilder every day.

The hunter knew he could not follow Red Ruff with a gun. So he set a row of traps across Red Ruff's feeding ground. These traps were made with young trees.

One day Red Ruff walked right into one. It jerked him into the air. There he hung by one foot.

All that day Red Ruff hung, beating his strong wings. He tried hard to get free. He tried all day and all night. Still he hung there. Then he wished for death to come. The second day wore on. Red Ruff was dying.

About midnight of the second night, a great horned owl heard Red Ruff's weak wings beat. The horned owl rushed in. The owl was far kinder than the man had been. It killed Red Ruff quickly.

Red, green, gold, and blue feathers rode on the wind that night. They dropped on the snow and on the ice.

That was the last night there were any such feathers, for Red Ruff was the last partridge of his kind. Partridges no longer come to that country. The old drumming log in the forest has rotted away.

PART 6

The SPRINGFIELD FOX

My uncle in Springfield had been losing hens for over a month. When I came to stay for the summer, my uncle asked me to find the robber. I saw that the hens were carried off one at a time, sometimes before, sometimes after, they went to roost.

This was not the work of a man, for the hens were never taken from high perches. Neither raccoons nor owls were robbing our henhouse. I knew this because no hen was left partly eaten on the ground. Neither weasels, nor skunks, nor minks could be blamed. This made me think that our chickens were being taken by a fox.

Near a pine wood on the other bank of the river, I found fox tracks and a chicken feather. I climbed the bank to look around. Just then I heard crows cawing loudly overhead. A fox was in the middle of the stream.

The crows were teasing him. They wanted him to drop the hen he held in his mouth. They hoped he would leave it for them to eat. When the fox saw me, he dropped the hen and ran into the woods.

I had been right. Our chicken robber was a fox. Since he wanted to carry the chicken back to his den, I knew he must have baby foxes there. That evening I took Ranger, my hound dog, and set out to find them.

It was not long before we heard the short, sharp bark of a fox. It came from the woods. Ranger ran into the woods at once. Soon his voice was far away as he chased the fox.

I waited nearly an hour for Ranger. At last he came back. He was panting after his long run in the summer heat. He lay down at my feet.

Almost at once I heard the fox bark, "Yap-yurrr!" He was very near us. Off went Ranger on another chase. He roared like a foghorn.

"Boo—boo—boo—!" he cried. "OO—oo—oo!"

He must have gone miles away, for his voice became more and more faint.

At last I heard Ranger's heavy breathing as he came back. He was tired. His tongue hung almost to the ground. He was dripping with foam. His sides rose and fell. He licked my hand. Then he flopped to the ground, panting noisily.

Again we heard the fox. This time I understood what had been happening. We were close to the den where the little foxes were. The old ones were taking turns trying to lead us away. It was late, so Ranger and I went back home.

SCARFACE AND HIS FAMILY

All the farmers knew that a fox and his family were living nearby. They called this fox Scarface because of a scar that reached from his eye to back of his ear. Everyone thought he had been caught on a barbed wire fence while chasing rabbits. White hair grew in this scar, so anyone who saw him remembered the mark.

Scarface was a clever fox. I had known of him since the spring before. A friend and I had been out hunting. We had passed close to some large gray and brown rocks.

"Stone number three looks like a fox curled up," said my friend.

"It just looks like a stone to me," I answered.

"I am sure that is a fox," my friend said. "I saw the wind blow his fur."

"We'll soon find out," I said, turning back.

As soon as I took one step from the road, up jumped Scarface. Away he ran. The strange part of this is not that Scarface looked like the stones, but that he *knew* he looked like them.

It was Scarface and his mate, Vixen, who were making our henhouse their food store.

The next morning I went to the pine woods to find Scarface's den. I found a bank of earth that had been scratched up in the past few months. I knew this dirt must have come from a hole. Yet I could find no hole.

A really clever fox has a trick to hide his den. He covers up the first hole he digs. Then he makes a tunnel under the ground to some bushes. There he makes another hole. The hole hidden in the bushes is the one he uses to get into his den.

On the hillside stood a large hollow tree. We boys had often played in it. We had cut steps in the trunk so we could easily get up and down. The next day, I climbed the hollow tree. I sat on the top. From there I could see the fox family.

There were four baby foxes. They had woolly coats, long black legs, and sweet faces. They looked like little lambs. But their sharp eyes showed that someday they would be sly foxes.

They played and rolled in the sunshine. Soon Vixen, their mother, stepped out of the bushes. She carried a hen. The little fellows ran to her. Then I saw something that I enjoyed very much. I knew my uncle would not have enjoyed it at all.

The baby foxes rushed at the hen. They snapped at it, and at one another. Vixen, keeping one eye open for enemies, watched them proudly.

I spent many days on top of the hollow tree watching the fox family. I watched Scarface and Vixen teach the babies to "freeze" and to kill small animals and birds.

One morning I saw them kill a woodchuck. This woodchuck lived on our hill. He was a dull fellow, but hard-working.

His den was between the roots of an old pine stump where the foxes could not get him. Each morning he sat on the stump in the sun. If a fox came near, he would go inside his den.

One morning the foxes wanted to teach their young ones about woodchucks. Vixen and Scarface went to the stump. Scarface walked slowly by the woodchuck's den.

When the woodchuck saw him, he went into his hole. When Scarface had passed, he came out. Just then Vixen leaped from behind the pine stump. She caught the woodchuck in her teeth and shook him until he was senseless.

Scarface came back. He watched proudly. Vixen carried the woodchuck back to her den. She called softly at the door.

The baby foxes came out, ready to play. Vixen threw the woodchuck on the ground. They jumped on him. They growled and bit him.

When he came to, he hit back, broke away, and limped into the bushes. The little ones went after him. They dragged at his tail and legs, but they could not hold him back.

Vixen got him in two jumps. She dragged him back into the open. The babies set on him again. One of the little foxes was badly bitten. He cried out with pain. Vixen got the woodchuck once more and quickly killed him for the little foxes to eat.

HOW TO CATCH FIELD MICE

Field mice lived in a grassy place near the foxes' den. One day Vixen took the little foxes to see the mice. There she gave them their first hunting lesson.

The little foxes lay in the grass to watch. They heard a noise. The lesson began.

Now, Vixen knew that tunnels where mice run are hidden under the high grass. She watched for moving grass. She knew she had to grab the mouse first and see him later.

Vixen stood on her back feet to see better. She jumped. She grabbed a bunch of grass. The field mouse in it squeaked, and she gobbled him down.

Then the four little foxes tried to follow their mother. The biggest got a mouse. It was the first time in his life he had ever done so. He shook with joy and sank his sharp teeth into the mouse.

THE RED-SQUIRREL GAME

Another time I saw the foxes learn about red squirrels. One of these noisy animals lived close to Scarface's den. The squirrel spent part of each day scolding the foxes. He shouted at them from a safe place. The foxes could not catch him as long as he stayed in the trees.

One day Vixen hid her little ones. Then she lay down in an open patch of grass. The squirrel ran up to a branch overhead. He scolded and scolded. Vixen did not move a hair. The squirrel came nearer. Could something be wrong with her?

"You brute, you! You brute, you!" he cried.

But Vixen lay still. The squirrel came down the tree trunk. He peeped around and ran across the grass to another tree.

"You brute, you!" he called.

Vixen did not move. The squirrel felt very brave. Again he ran across the grass. He came even nearer to Vixen. He dropped a piece of bark on Vixen's head.

The squirrel had used up his list of bad names. He had scolded and scolded. But she had not showed a sign of life. He became braver and braver.

He made two or three more runs across the grassy spot. Each time he came a little nearer. At last he came right up to the waiting fox. She grabbed him and held him with one foot.

The little ones picked on his bones.

MORE LESSONS FOR LITTLE FOXES

I watched the fox family each day. I never told my uncle how I spent my time.

When the little foxes were older, Vixen took them farther from home. They learned more about hunting.

They learned that every animal has some way to save itself. If it did not, it could not live. Every animal also has some weakness. If it did not, other animals would not be able to live.

Here are some of the lessons the foxes learned:

Trust your nose before your eyes.

Running water hides many things.

Never go in the open if you can keep hidden.

Never leave a straight trail if you can leave a crooked one.

Anything strange is your enemy.

Dust and water hide your smell.

Keep off the grass.

If you can't smell it, then the wind must be so that it can smell you.

The little foxes learned their lessons. They were sure they knew the smell of everything in the world. Then one night Vixen took them to a strange thing on the ground. It was a man's coat. When they smelled it, the foxes shook with fear. "This is man-smell!" Vixen said.

SCARFACE FOOLS RANGER

All this time we were losing hens from our henhouse. I had not told my uncle about the den. Indeed, I liked the foxes better than I liked the hens.

My uncle was very angry. Every day he said bad things about me as a fox hunter. One day, to please him, I took Ranger with me. We went to the woods. I sat on a stump and told Ranger to go on. In a few minutes he barked, "Fox! Fox! Fox!"

Soon I heard the foxes coming. Scarface ran toward the stream and jumped into the water. He ran along in the water for about two hundred yards. He was watching over his shoulder for the dog and didn't see me. When he was only ten feet away from me, he stopped.

Ranger ran along the trail. When he came to the water, he stopped. He went up and down both sides of the brook, trying to find where the fox had left the stream.

Old Scarface watched the hound. Scarface was so close to me that I could see the hair on his shoulder rise when Ranger came near.

The dog was fooled by the water trick. Scarface could not sit still. He rocked up and down in joy. He stood up on his back feet to see the hound. With mouth opened nearly to his ears, he seemed to laugh.

Then he stole quietly away into the woods. His life had been in my hands, but he never knew it. Ranger would have passed me also. I spoke to him. With a little jump, he came toward me and lay down by my feet.

THE END OF SCARFACE

This went on for days. My uncle got even angrier. He hated to lose his hens. One day he took his gun and sat on the hill. Scarface trotted out. My uncle shot him in the back.

But still the hens were taken! Vixen was on the job.

My uncle put out poisoned bait. He hoped that our own dogs would not get it. He made fun of me for failing to catch the chicken-stealing foxes. Every night he went out with a gun and two dogs to hunt foxes.

Vixen went right by the poison bait without touching it. She picked up one piece and dropped it down the hole of her old enemy, the skunk. He was never seen again.

When Scarface was alive, he had taken care of the dogs. Now Vixen had to do everything. She no longer had time to fool all the enemies that might be near.

DIGGING OUT THE DEN OF FOXES

Ranger and Spot, the little dog, were running in the woods. Ranger found the foxes' den. Spot barked to say that the whole family was at home. He did his best to go into the hole after them.

The whole story was out. Paddy, the hired man, came to dig the foxes out. The dogs stood by. Vixen soon showed up in the nearby woods. She led the dogs to the river and lost them.

The trick she used was a good one. She jumped onto a sheep's back. The sheep ran for about a hundred yards. Then Vixen jumped off again. There was a break in the trail. She knew the dogs could not find her, and she went back to her den.

The dogs soon got back to the den, also. They found her there, trying to get us away from her babies. Paddy worked hard with his pick and spade. The dirt piled higher on both sides. He dug for more than an hour. Then he called, "Here they are!"

The four cubs were as far back in the den as they could get. They were very much afraid.

Before I could say a word, Paddy lifted his spade. With one blow he killed three of the baby foxes. I saved the smallest one by holding him up by the tail, away from the dogs.

The poor, scared, little fox gave a little cry. His mother came near. But she kept out of our reach. The three dead little brothers were buried in the ground. The live one was dropped into a sack. He lay still.

LITTLE TIP IN CHAINS

We chained the little fox in the back yard. We named him Tip. He was a pretty little fellow. No one wanted to kill him.

He was very unhappy. As long as anyone was near, he stayed in his box. At night he bit his chain and cried.

One night from far away came Vixen's "Yap-yurrrr." A few minutes later, she stood by the woodpile. The little one ran to meet his mother. Vixen grabbed him. She turned and started off. When she reached the end of his chain, the cub was jerked from her mouth. Someone opened a window, and she was scared away by the sound.

An hour later, the cub was still. I peeped out of my window. I saw Vixen on the ground beside her little one. She was biting Tip's chain. While she lay there, the little one was nursing. She left two freshly-killed mice next to Tip's box.

Next day I went past the den. I could see that Vixen had come back. She had dug out the bodies of her three little ones and had licked them clean. Beside them were two of our hens.

Deep prints showed where she had lain. But after a while, she went no more to the den. She surely knew the babies were dead.

VIXEN'S FIGHT FOR TIP

Tip had all of Vixen's love. My uncle let the dogs loose at night to guard the hen-house. The hired man had orders to shoot the old fox. I had orders, too. But I made up my mind never to see her. Poisoned chicken heads had been thrown about. A fox loves chicken heads, but a dog will not touch them.

The only way Vixen could get to Tip was by climbing the woodpile. Before she could do that she had to pass many other dangers. Yet she came every night. She was always near.

One night the dogs made a lot of noise. They tore away through the woods. They were chasing Vixen. They went north toward the railroad track. Next morning Ranger had not come back.

Foxes know how to use a railroad track to get the best of their enemies. Sometimes they walk the rails for a long way when the train is coming. The train wipes out their trail. Sometimes the hound is killed by the train.

Sometimes a fox leads the hounds to a high bridge just ahead of the train. The train overtakes the hounds on the bridge. They fall through and are killed on the rocks below. Vixen played this trick on Ranger.

That night she killed another hen before Spot could stop her. She took the hen to Tip. Then she lay beside him so he could nurse. She seemed to think that the only food he had was what she got for him.

My uncle found out that Vixen had come when he saw the dead hen. Otherwise he might never have known. I would never have told him. I was very sorry for Vixen now.

My uncle tried to shoot Vixen. But three times he failed. Would she come again?

On the fourth night, I was the only one to watch. I saw Vixen climb over the woodpile. She was not carrying a chicken. Had her hunting failed? Had she learned that we would feed Tip?

Vixen had learned that she could not free Tip. She had braved every danger to care for him. She had tried her best to break his chain. But she had failed.

She dropped something near Tip. Then she was gone. Tip grabbed what she had brought. It was a chicken head! He bit on it and chewed it. Even as he ate, he screamed with pain. Then the little fox lay dead.

Vixen's love for Tip was strong. Even stronger was her love of freedom. She had to choose for him between death or a prisoner's life. She set him free in the only way she knew.

Vixen left our woods. Where she went, I never knew.

PART 7

ℭhe PACING MUSTANG

Wild Joe Calone threw his saddle on the dusty ground. He turned his horses loose. Then he went into the ranch house. His spurs jingled as he walked.

"About lunch time?" he asked. "This New Mexico air makes me hungry!"

"Seventeen minutes," said the cook, old Turkey-Track. He looked at his watch.

"How is everything on the ranch?" asked Scarth, Joe's partner.

"Cows seem O.K.," answered Joe. "Lots of young ones."

"I saw that bunch of mustangs that water at Antelope Springs," said Scarth. "Two or three colts were along. One is little and dark. He's a dandy, a born pacer."

"Is that so?" asked Joe. "A born pacer?"

"I ran them for a mile or two," Scarth said. "That little horse led the bunch all the way. He never broke his pace."

"Too bad you had to come back to eat!" said Joe, jokingly.

"That's all right, Joe. I'll get another chance."

"Chuck!" cried Turkey-Track.

The ranch hands went in for dinner. The talk about the little pacer was dropped. Next day the camp moved. The band of wild horses was forgotten.

WILD JOE SEES THE LITTLE BLACK PACER

A year later at branding time, the men were once again rounding up calves. Again the men saw the wild herd.

The dark colt was now a black yearling. His thin legs were long and clean; his coat shiny. He was strong. The cowboys could see that the yearling was indeed a born pacer.

Wild Joe was along this time. When he saw the black yearling, he wanted it for his own.

Most cowboys don't take time to catch wild horses. In the first place, they are hard to catch. And once you have them, they are very hard to tame. Some cattle ranchers shoot mustangs to keep them from eating the grass on the range or, even worse, from leading away the ranchers' tame horses.

"I never saw a white horse that wasn't soft," Joe said. "I never saw a chestnut that wasn't nervous. I never saw a bay that wasn't a good horse if you broke him right. And I never saw a black that wasn't as hard as nails and full of life."

"What about mustangs?" asked Scarth. "Does that go for them, too?"

"A mustang?" asked Joe. "All a mustang needs is claws to be wilder than a den of lions. Mustangs are no good. And a black mustang is ten times worse than no good. But still I'd like to have that little black!"

"If black mustangs are such bad horses, why do you want him?" asked Scarth.

"Why do I want him?" asked Joe. "I guess because I'm kind of a wild fellow myself."

THE BLACK PACER GROWS UP

Joe Calone had no chance to catch the little pacer that year. Joe was only a cowpuncher. His hours were long, and his pay was small. Like most cowboys, he hoped someday to own his own ranch. But each fall when he got his pay, he would go to town with the other cowboys. His money would soon be gone, and he would go back to work without a penny.

The only things Joe owned were his saddle and his bedroll. He kept thinking about the little black mustang. If he had the pacer for his own, his luck might change. If only he had a chance to catch him!

The roundup of calves lasted through the summer until late in the fall. Joe sometimes heard about the pacing mustang, but he saw no more of him. The black colt was now a fast, young, wild horse. He was almost three years old. Many people were talking about him.

Antelope Springs, Joe learned, was the place the horse liked best. It was the only drinking place for miles around. It was in the middle of a large flat piece of land. Many herds of range horses and cattle came there for water.

A man named Foster was manager and part owner of the L CROSS F cattle outfit. He was trying to build up better herds of horses and cattle in that part of New Mexico. He had ten beautiful mares.

Foster kept one of these fine mares at the ranch for his own use. The other nine mares had run away from the ranch and had gone twenty miles south to Antelope Springs.

Late in the summer Foster went to round them up. With them he found the coal-black pacer. The pacer had taken the mares for his own and was guarding them. His jet-black coat looked even more beautiful among the golden coats of his mares.

Foster's nine mares were gentle enough. He thought it would be easy to round them up and take them home. But he had not figured on the pacer. When the wild black horse saw Foster, he started to move. Running this way and that, he rounded up the little band of mares. Then, at a full gallop, he drove the whole band away! Foster and Joe, on their little cow ponies, were soon left far behind. Both men took out their guns.

They tried to shoot the pacer, but there was no chance.

All day long the two men chased the horses. But the pacer kept his family together. At last they were gone, lost in the sand hills. There was nothing else for the tired men to do but start for home.

"I guess you have lost nine good mares," said Joe.

"Maybe I have," Foster said, "but someday I'll catch up with that black devil."

A wild male horse often has a large following of mares. The great black horse and his large band of mares were seen in many places.

He added mares from the nearby ranches to his band. Before long he had twenty in his herd. Foster's nine mares were the best of the lot. The black horse guarded them well. No man could get near them, no matter how hard he tried.

I SET OUT TO GET THE PACING MUSTANG

I was new in the ranch country of New Mexico that winter. I was working for Foster at the L cross F outfit. Just before I started out with my wagon, Foster said, "Shoot that black mustang if you get a chance."

As Jack Burns and I rode along, he told me about the black mustang. I could not wait to see him.

On the third day out, we came to the Antelope Springs country. We still had not seen any sign of the pacer and his band. Burns was riding ahead. I was driving the wagon. Suddenly Burns dropped flat on the neck of his horse.

"Get your rifle!" he yelled. "Here's the black pacer!"

I grabbed my rifle, jumped out of the wagon, and hurried over a little hill which was ahead of us.

Just below us was a band of horses. With them was the great black mustang. He had heard us. He smelled danger. There he stood, as fine a horse as I had ever seen. No such animal had ever before been seen on the plains.

I could not think of killing that horse.

"Shoot quickly!" said Jack. But I could not shoot.

"Here! Give it to me!" he cried. The gun went off as he grabbed it, but the shot went wild.

The great black leader snorted. He dashed about, rounding up the mares. Away they went in a cloud of dust.

The black mustang galloped from one side to another, driving the mares. He kept his eye on all of them. And he kept his eye on Jack and me. Never once did he break his beautiful pace!

Jack was very angry with me. He said I had let the gun go off so the horses could get away. Jack was also angry with the black mustang. But I was not. I loved that horse as soon as I saw him. I would not have hurt him for all the mares in the bunch.

JOE TRIES TO GET THE BLACK MUSTANG

There are three or four ways to get a wild horse. One is by grazing his neck with a bullet. This stops him until you can tie him up.

"None of that for me!" said Wild Joe Calone. "I've seen about a hundred horses with their necks broken that way."

120

Another way is to drive the herd into a corral. Another is to run the horse down. The best way is to walk the horse down.

The black mustang and his pacing had become known to all the ranchers and cowboys.

"I'll give one thousand dollars cash for that black horse. Get him safe in a boxcar, and the money is yours!" said old Montgomery, the owner of another outfit.

A dozen young cowpunchers had heard about this offer. They all wanted to win the money. Just as soon as their work was ended, they planned to catch the black pacer.

Wild Joe Calone had other ideas. He had wanted that horse himself for a long time. Now there was no more time to lose.

Joe got a little money here and there. He got some horses and a chuck wagon, too. He even got some food. He, a cowboy named Charley, and the cook, old Turkey-Track, were going to walk the mustang down.

WALKING DOWN THE PACER—THE START

On their third day out, the three men came to Antelope Springs. There they found the pacing mustang and his band of mares.

Joe hid. He wanted the horses to drink their fill. A horse full of water is a poor runner. Joe gave them all the time they wanted at the spring.

Then Joe rode quietly forward. The pacer saw him a half mile away. He rounded up his band. He led them away, heading south. Joe went after them at a gallop. Soon he saw the band again. Then he rode back.

"We can cut them off. Head to the south!" he told old Turkey-Track.

Then Joe himself set out southeast, following the herd of horses. After a mile or two, he saw them again. He walked his horse up quietly. When he neared the band, they again ran south.

Joe cut across to head them off. When he could see them again, he walked his horse quietly toward them. Again they set off at a run.

The afternoon passed. The mustang and his band headed farther and farther to the south. At last they were not far from where Turkey-Track was. Then Joe cut across again. This time he rode to the wagon. Charley was waiting to take up the walking chase on a fresh horse.

After supper Joe and Turkey-Track camped for the night. Charley followed the herd. The horses were getting used to a man riding up on a horse. They were no longer afraid of him.

After the sun went down, the men could still follow the herd. One of the mares was white. On and on rode Charley. Then, in the darkest night, Charley lost them. He got off his horse, rolled up in his blanket, and fell asleep on the ground.

Charley was up at the first light of dawn. Less than half a mile away, he found the band. When the horses saw him, off they ran. But then they stopped to look back.

For a moment or so, they stood watching Charley. Then the black mustang turned. He wanted to get rid of the man. With his black mane flying, he led off in his even, beautiful pace. The mares followed him.

Away they went to the west. The same game went on: run, follow, overtake, cut across, run again. By noon they had come to where Joe sat with the wagon.

"Now it's my turn," Joe said.

Charley sat down to eat and to rest. Turkey-Track moved the camp to the next spot. All that day Joe followed the band of horses. The camp wagon took a short cut while the mustang and his band went the long way around.

At sundown Joe met Charley waiting with another fresh horse for him. Joe changed horses. He followed the herd all evening and far into the night.

The mares were getting tired. They had been on the run for a long time. They were no longer in the good grass country. Joe's horses were fed grain. The herd had only grass. The horses were very thirsty, too. Joe let the herd fill up with water at every chance. Everybody knows that it is not good for running animals to drink. It makes their legs stiff and hurts their breathing.

THE NEXT FEW DAYS

Joe was up at dawn. The wild horses were not far away. At first they ran. Soon they slowed down to a walk. The race seemed to be almost won.

All that morning Joe kept near the pacer and his mares. Then Charley took over. That day the mustangs moved much more slowly. They began to turn more to the north.

On the next day, the tired animals walked with their heads down. Sometimes they were only a hundred yards ahead of Charley.

After the fifth day, the tired herd was almost back to Antelope Springs. Everything had gone as Joe wanted. The horses had moved in a big ring. The wagon had followed in a small ring.

The pacer and his mares reached Antelope Springs. They were worn out. Joe and Charley were also back, on fresh horses. The men kept the herd from drinking until late afternoon. Then they drove the horses to the water. When the horses had filled up with water, Joe and Charley planned to close in. The only thing wrong with this plan was the black mustang. He seemed to be made of iron. His pace seemed as swift and strong as it had been on the very first morning.

Up and down he went, trying to get the mares to run away. The tired mares could not go. But the prize of all the hunt, the black pacer, was still out of Joe's reach.

THE END OF THE CHASE

During that week Joe had never seen the mustang gallop. Not once had he broken his long, easy pacing. Joe's love for the black horse had grown and grown. He would as soon shoot his best friend as shoot that horse.

The time had now come to end the hunt. Joe got his best horse. She was Joe's own horse, an eastern mare raised on the plains. There was only one thing wrong with her. She was loco—crazy.

Loco weed, which contains a poison, grows in the West. Most horses and cattle will not eat it. The weed acts like a drug, and any horse that eats it goes mad. Joe's horse had eaten loco weed. He knew that someday she would go mad. Still, she was fast and strong. Joe chose her for the end of the chase.

It was easy enough to get the tired mares away from their black leader. It would be easy, now, to take them back to the L CROSS

F Ranch. But the black pacer was still strong and wild. Here was a job for Wild Joe Calone.

First Joe worked over his rope. Then he spurred his horse. He rode right at the pacer, who stood a fourth of a mile away. Away they went. The fresh horse ran at her fastest gallop. But the mustang held his lead. He did not break his pace.

Joe could not believe his eyes. He spurred his horse and shouted. She fairly flew. But he could not gain one inch on the black mustang. The pacer flew across the flats, across the sandy plains, across the grass. He began to leave the mare behind.

Suddenly the mare's eyes began to roll. She shook her head wildly from side to side. Her foot went into a hole. Down she went! Joe flew over her head and hit the ground, hard.

Joe got to his feet. Then he saw that the mare's leg was broken. There was only one thing for him to do. Joe shot the mare. Then, carrying his saddle, he set out for camp. Away ran the mustang. Soon he was out of sight.

The trip was not for nothing. Joe and Charley drove the mares back. They got good pay from Foster. But, more than ever, Joe wanted to catch the black mustang.

Joe was not the only one who wanted to own the black pacer. Old Turkey-Track also wanted him.

"Well, I saw that pacer today," said Horseshoe Billy, one of the cowhands. "He was so near I could have shot off an inch of his tail."

"Why didn't you shoot?" asked one of the cowboys.

"I'll tell you why he didn't shoot that mustang," said Charley. "He knew he couldn't hit it!"

"Don't believe that," said Horseshoe Billy. "That horse will carry my brand before the moon changes!"

"I don't think he will," said Charley, "because I mean to catch him myself."

"Where did you see him?" asked Turkey-Track.

"Well, it was like this," said Billy. "I was riding the flat land by Antelope Springs. All at once I saw the pacer lying asleep in the bushes. There he was. I thought he was dead until I saw his ear move. Well, my rope was an old one and not much good. I knew I couldn't hold him with that. So I just hit the saddle horn with my rope. I wish you'd seen that mustang. He jumped six feet in the air with his eyes sticking out. Then he took off for California. He should be there by now, the way he started."

Billy did not tell lies. Everyone believed this story. Old Turkey-Track said nothing. He had a new idea.

OLD TOM TURKEY-TRACK'S PLAN

After dinner Turkey-Track took his pipe outdoors. He sat on a box and thought for a long time. He had a plan, but he needed a partner. He could not do this alone.

That evening he found Horseshoe Billy. He told Billy his plan. The two would try to get the pacer and the thousand dollars.

The water at Antelope Springs was low. There was a broad strip of black mud around the water. Two trails crossed this mud strip. It was on one of these trails that Horseshoe

Billy and old Turkey-Track wanted to set a trap for the pacer. They went to work and dug a pit fifteen feet long, six feet wide, and seven feet deep. It took them many hours of hard work.

When the pit was done, the men covered it with poles, brush, and dirt. Then they hid, to wait for the pacer.

He came about noon. He was alone. He did not take the right path as he walked down to the water. He put down his head and took a good drink.

Turkey-Track ran down the trail behind the pacer. He took out his gun and fired a shot into the ground.

Away ran the horse, heading right for the trap! Another second and he would have been in it. But, with a mighty leap, he jumped over the fifteen-foot trap and got away. He was never seen to use either trail again.

WILD JOE HAS ANOTHER PLAN

Wild Joe had still not given up. He wanted to try a relay chase.

The black mustang ran within a big triangle of land. It was marked off by a river, some hills, and a creek. Joe knew this country well. He also knew the pacer's ways. He got twenty good horses and five good riders for the relay chase.

The day before the relay, the grain-fed horses were sent on ahead. On the day of the relay, Joe drove his wagon to the plain near Antelope Springs. There he waited.

At last the pacer came. He was alone. He walked down to the spring and drank.

Joe was watching. He spurred his horse. The pacer heard the hoofs. Then he saw the running horse. He took off to the south across the flat. Again he kept his even pace. Soon Joe's horse was far behind.

Into the sand hills the mustang went. Joe's horse ran through the loose sand, losing ground at every step. On and on they went. They rode one mile—two miles—three miles. Far ahead were the rocks. Joe had fresh horses waiting there.

Joe reached the place where a fresh horse was waiting for him. He jumped on it. Then he set out after the flying pacer. But not an inch did he gain!

One hour—two hours—three hours passed. Just ahead waited another fresh horse. The black mustang raced ahead. Then, for some reason, he turned to the left. Joe tried to head him off. This was the hardest race of all. Joe's horse panted for breath.

Joe took out his gun and fired shot after shot. He wanted to turn the mustang. He was trying to make him take the crossing at the right.

Down went Joe's horse; he was done for. Thirty miles had ended him. Joe was worn-out, too. His eyes burned from the sandy dust.

"Keep him going straight!" he told his next relay partner.

Out shot a fresh rider on a fresh horse. Away they went, up and down the rolling plain. The black mustang was covered with snowy sweat. Still on and on he went.

At first the new rider seemed to gain. Then he began to lose. They came to a long hill. There another fresh rider on another fresh horse took up the chase.

The mustang was now covered with dust and sweat. He now looked brown instead of black. But his pace stayed the same. Young Carrington, the last rider, spurred his horse to jump a ditch. The pacer had already jumped over. Carrington's horse missed it by an inch. The boy was safe, but the pony lay dead at the bottom. And the wild black horse kept right on!

Thirty minutes later, Joe himself once again was on the pacer's trail. He had another fresh horse. Far in the west, Joe could see the hills where he knew more men and fresh horses were waiting. He tried to turn the pacer. But the mustang turned to the north instead.

Joe rode and yelled and shot his gun. The wild black horse ran down a ditch. The only thing Joe could do was to follow him.

Now came the hardest part of the race. The sun was hot. Joe's eyes and lips burned with sand and salt. His only chance was to drive the mustang back. Now, for the first time, he saw signs that the black was getting weaker. His lead was half what it had been. Still he stayed ahead. And still he kept his pace.

Another hour and still another hour passed. Joe wanted to be the one to ride the last twenty miles of the relay. He jumped on the waiting horse. The horse he left went to the stream. There it filled itself with water until it dropped dead.

Joe held back, in case the mustang wanted a drink. But the wild horse was wise. As he leaped through the water, he took only one fast drink. Then he went on. The black was ahead, just out of Joe's reach.

Next morning Joe came walking into camp. His story was short. Eight horses were dead. Five men were worn-out. The pacer was still free.

"That horse can't be caught!" said Joe.

OLD TURKEY-TRACK TRIES AGAIN

Old Turkey-Track had watched Joe's relay race. We were all talking about it. It was all anyone could talk about.

"That mustang is mine," said Turkey-Track, when the relay race failed. "He's mine, or I'm a fool!"

"You're a fool all right!" said Slim. "But that horse is no fool!"

134

"No, he's not," said Turkey-Track. "But he does have one weakness. You'll see."

The pacer was now wilder than ever. He knew that he was hunted. But he still came to Antelope Springs almost every day about noon.

The pacing mustang had been alone all winter. Old Turkey-Track knew this. So he got a brown mare. Then he rode away to Antelope Springs. With him he carried a pair of strong hobbles, a spade, an extra rope, and a strong post.

The day was cool and fresh. The cattle lay around in little bands. The sweet songs of the birds were everywhere. The grass was turning green. Spring was at hand.

Old Turkey-Track tied up the little brown mare where she could eat grass. She raised her nose from time to time. She called out as if she wanted company.

Turkey-Track watched and waited. He looked at the pit he had dug before. It had filled with water. Turkey-Track picked out a good spot and put the post into the ground. Then he dug himself a hole to hide in. He laid his blanket in it. Then he laid his rope on the ground. He tied one end of the rope to the post. He covered the rope with dust and grass and went back to his hiding place.

About noon the mustang came. There he stood on a high spot, black against the sky. He had heard the call of the little brown mare.

Down he came, stopping often to look and to listen.

The brown mare called again. He came closer still. His fears were forgotten. He came up and touched her nose with his own.

Suddenly his hind legs were caught in Turkey-Track's rope. The black mustang was caught at last!

Snorting in fear, he jumped into the air. Tom Turkey-Track pulled the rope. Down went the mustang, flat on his side.

Old Tom Turkey-Track came out of the pit. The black snorted and kicked. He tried to break loose, but the strong rope held.

Turkey-Track swung a second rope. It caught the black's front feet. Then the man pulled the pacer's feet together. The pacer was tied on the ground. He kicked until he was worn-out.

Tom stood by. When the horse stopped fighting, Turkey-Track put the hobbles on him. Then Turkey-Track remembered something. According to the law of the West, a mustang belonged to the first man to brand him. He must brand the great black pacer. But the nearest branding iron was twenty miles away!

Old Tom went over to the mare. He pulled off her loose shoe. Then he built a fire. Soon he had one arm of the horseshoe red-hot.

With the red-hot shoe, he put his brand on the pacer's left shoulder. The helpless mustang had been branded for the first time. On its shoulder was a mark like a turkey track. The pacer screamed as the hot iron burned him. It was all over in a few minutes. The famous mustang now belonged to Tom.

Tom loosened the ropes. For a moment the mustang thought he was free. He sprang to his feet.

Then he found he could not step. He fell as soon as he tried to walk. His front feet were tied together. The only way he could move was to jump along. Each time he tried to break away, he fell.

Tom got onto the mare. He tried his best to drive the pacer home. But the black would not give in. He snorted in fear and anger. He fought to get free. His shiny coat was covered with sweat and blood. The many hard falls were beginning to show on him. Old Tom still drove him on.

At last they got near the ranch buildings. Old Turkey-Track was tired. The mustang used all the strength he had left to make one more try. Up, up the grassy hill he jumped. Turkey-Track swung a rope at him. He fired his gun into the air. He tried to turn the mustang back.

On jumped the black mustang. He stood above the highest cliff for a moment. Then he jumped into air. Down he fell—two hundred feet to the rocks below. He lay at the bottom, broken and lifeless, but free.